AN ESSENT
NEW FATHER AN

From the myst
of the labour ward; from post-natal depression (yours) to the never-before-revealed secrets to a good night's sleep, this guide gives the new father vital advice on keeping his nerve, friends and job at a time of unparalleled upheaval.

STRICTLY NOT TO BE SOLD TO, GIVEN TO, OR READ BY, MOTHERS OR PREGNANT WOMEN

FATHERHOOD . . .
THE AWFUL TRUTH!

FATHERHOOD . . . THE AWFUL TRUTH!

NIGEL FARRELL
Cartoons by Trevor Ricketts

JAVELIN BOOKS
POOLE · NEW YORK · SYDNEY

First published in the UK 1987 by Javelin Books,
Link House, West Street, Poole, Dorset, BH15 1LL

Distributed in the United States by
Sterling Publishing Co., Inc.,
2 Park Avenue, New York, NY 10016

Distributed in Australia by
Capricorn Link (Australia) Pty Ltd,
PO Box 665, Lane Cove, NSW 2066

British Library Cataloguing in Publication Data

Farrel, Nigel
1. Fatherhood: the awful truth
1. Fathers—Anecdotes, Facetiae, Satire, etc
I. Title
306.8'742'0207 HQ756

ISBN 0 7137 1897 8

Typeset by Butler & Tanner Ltd, Frome and London.
Printed in Great Britain by Cox & Wyman Ltd,
London and Reading

Never throw stones at your mother,
You'll be sorry for it when she's dead,
Never throw stones at your mother,
Throw bricks at your father instead.

Brendan Behan

CONTENTS

The author wishes to express his thanks for permission to use extracts from the following: *The Case For Reincarnation* by Joe Fisher, published by Granada Publishing Limited, and *Magic, Myth and Medicine* by John Camp, published by Priory Press Limited.

INTRODUCTION

It was two or three minutes before the birth of my first child that the awful significance of what was about to happen suddenly hit me.

We were alone in the small, blindingly-white delivery room. My wife lay in anguish beside me, pleading for more ice-cubes and squeezing my hand, as she had been for the past hour, with the applied grip of a mechanical pulping machine. The midwife had gone out for a moment, handing me, as she left, a small face-mask attached to a cylinder of nitrous oxide.

'If she gets out of control, love, give her a squirt of that to calm her down', she said matter-of-factly as she left.

Standing there in my surgical gown I felt my knees begin to wobble violently. Was it really too late to back out now? What was I doing here anyway? Who were all these people wandering round in blood-spattered face-masks? Who was I? And why do I keep asking myself bloody silly questions?

At any moment now a brand new human being would emerge. The prospect was quite terrifying. Suddenly, in a moment of blind panic, I felt right out of my depth.

There seemed only one thing to do. Using the hand not at present in the process of being pulped, I reached for the cylinder of gas and air and pushed the face-mask over my nose and mouth, inhaling deeply, and with feeling.

My toes tingled.

I inhaled again, with more feeling. Gradually the tingling worked its way from my toes upwards, and after a time I found myself gently floating around the room like a vast hot-air balloon on a warm and lazy air current. Perhaps life wasn't so bad after all. It was as if I was breathing-in the cool, sweet-smelling scent of a late summer's evening after hay-making. I could see bowls of strawberries stretched out before me. In my hand was a glass of sparkling champagne. In my ears a choir of archangels was singing a Hallelujah chorus.

Slowly I became aware of the well-rounded shape of the midwife peering at me. 'Everything all right in here?' I heard her ask, with a degree of suspicion.

'Yes', I managed to say, at length, and I noticed with horror as I spoke that my voice had shot into an anguished falsetto with the effect of the gas and air so that I sounded like Mickey Mouse. 'Yes, yes, thank you, I feel much better now.'

'I didn't mean you,' she snapped. 'I meant your wife, and – ' here she paused abruptly, nodding down ' – and your child.'

I looked down, too. I could just make out a tiny pale circle of dark hair about to make its spectacular debut.

Life has simply never been the same since.

* * *

I once came across a doctor who carried out a vasectomy on himself. He went into his own surgery one day, sat down and, with his wife handing him over the vital pieces of gear, such as scalpels and so on, snipped away. It was all over in ten minutes.

Personally I find this approach a bit extreme. I mean I know children *en masse* have a pretty poor reputation amongst some adults but I would have thought that, in many cases, they are preferable to having to sit on a chair and hack away at your own vas deferens. And what on earth would have happened if at that moment the man had arrived to read the meter?

For most of us, of course, the question: 'Do we want children, if so, how many, and when?' is laughably academic. Does ANYBODY really make a decision about children that way and stick to it? In my experience the little blighters make up their own minds on such matters and simply arrive as and when they feel like it.

According to the Medical Research Council, man is 10,000 times more sexually prolific than the much-maligned rabbit, performing an estimated 1,000 million acts of sexual intercourse each year (yes, my mind boggled too) and producing 720,000 babies annually in Britain alone. This proves two things: firstly, that the phrase 'They're at it like rabbits' is now completely out of date and, secondly, that anyone with enough time to work out that kind of useless statistic obviously hasn't got children of his own.

Of course, the desire to procreate is supremely dominant amongst all levels of the animal kingdom. When male lions get going they copulate up to one hundred times every twenty-four hours, although the sexual act itself would seem to be rather unsatisfactory, lasting only about a minute. The record for copulation is held by a rodent, called a jird, that lives in the desert and has a sexual stamina which would have had even Casanova casting envious glances: the jird was observed copulating two hundred and twenty-four times in two hours, although frankly I feel that any zoologist who actually earns a living voyeuristically grubbing around the

ACCORDING TO THE MEDICAL RESEARCH COUNCIL, MAN IS 10,000 TIMES MORE SEXUALLY PROLIFIC THAN THE MUCH MALIGNED RABBIT.

sand dunes of the desert counting how many times jirds make love needs some kind of psychiatric help.

There is a sort of minute octopus-like creature, called a paper argonaut, which gets round this problem by having a detachable male organ. When a willing female paper argonaut is feeling ready for a night of passion she shouts out the argonautical equivalent of 'Chuck it over, darling!' and, like an Exocet missile, the male organ sets off all on its own, packed with sperm and ready for action.

My mother used to own a small poodle called Goldie, a cheerful enough little chap who, while still in possession of his male organ, had unfortunately been forced to part company with his testicles a long time before he had come into our ownership. This lack of vital equipment didn't seem to bother him in the least, that is, until the day mother bought home another poodle, this time a very large female called Evo who happened, rather unfortunately as it turned out, to be on heat.

Despite his past history, Goldie felt nevertheless that, if Evo was on heat, then the time had come to do his duty and the very first thing he did when they met was to mount her and get stuck in. Over the next few days we tried to keep them apart but the urge to be as one was so great that, however much we barricaded them into different rooms in the house, one or the other always seemed to be able to escape and within seconds they would be at it like billy-o. You may find it hard to believe, given his physiological condition, that Goldie was able to get going, but get going he did, plugging straight into Evo the moment he set eyes on her.

The problem, however, was that, while he seemed capable of carrying out the first part of the act, his castration meant he couldn't bring it to any kind of satisfactory conclusion. The poor animal kept at it hour after hour, much to Evo's obvious delight – that was the first and last time I've ever seen a dog actually smile – and eventually the wretched creature rubbed all the hair off his tummy so that his entire undercarriage was red and raw. He may not have had much style but when it came to perseverance I take my hat off to that little dog.

Offspring, of course, offer the gift of eternal life, the knowledge that, with luck, part of you will continue through the generations long after you as an individual are six foot under. The thought that you are a link in a chain, rather than an isolated, rather lonely little blob of scrap metal, the like of which the world will never see again, somehow makes the whole thing worthwhile. Poor Goldie.

Mind you, it is possible to overdo things. In the eighteenth century, a Russian peasant called Feodor Vassilyer was so concerned about his link in the chain that he married a woman who proceeded to give him sixty-nine children, the greatest officially-recorded number of children ever produced by any one woman. All but two of the children, comprising sixteen pairs of twins, seven sets of triplets and four sets of quadruplets, survived, although the good Mrs Vassilyer's state of mind and body after spending forty years suckling sixty-seven babies isn't recorded. She finally gave up the ghost and died, at which point F. Vassilyer Esq. promptly re-married and started up the whole ghastly business all over again.

No, our fertility seems obstinately pre-destined; all you can do is sit back and admire nature at work and make sure you have come to terms with the implications. Never again will you actually be in control of your own life, never again master of your own destiny. Your friends will change. Your wife will change. Your habits will change. Your home will change. Your bank balance will change. And, whether you like it or not, you will change, too; possibly, although I'll reserve judgement on this, for the better.

Anyway, let's get down to the nitty-gritty. You need to concentrate on preparing yourself for an event which, after your own birth, is probably the most dramatic and far-reaching you are ever likely to witness. You must devote yourself to removing as much of the unnecessary pain of fatherhood as possible and make damn sure that, while you may emerge from the experience a bit bashed about and unsteady on the old pins, you manage to retain at least some of your faculties.

Modern anthropologists argue that, in our fast-moving, stressful world we have a lot to learn from primitive man, and I must say that, when it comes to something called the Couvade Syndrome, I couldn't agree more. At one time the Couvade Syndrome could be found in primitive tribes all over the world, and it still exists in a few today. It describes a convention which begins when the wife of a tribesman becomes pregnant. Instead of the woman retiring to bed to gather her strength, the man does so. It is to the husband, not the wife, that gifts are brought. Despite getting bigger and more uncomfortable as the months draw by, the wife has to slave away as per normal, harvesting, cooking, and cleaning, whilst relatives and friends queue up at the door to bring the old man in bed flowers, make him nice hot cups of tea and keep fluffing up his pillows to make sure he is always comfy. The husband's lack of activity during the pregnancy is thought to be in direct proportion to the affection in which he holds his wife, so complete prostration is regarded as evidence of true and undying love.

Sounds reasonable enough to me.

The man, if he is really doing his stuff, may even show certain symptoms of pregnancy, such as exhaustion, cravings for yeast extract or stewed mice droppings, finishing off nine months later by acting out the birth itself, and then actually having an extended period of convalescence to recuperate.

All the woman has to do is simply to have the baby.

Now, whatever ideas you may have at the moment about your impending fatherhood, perhaps it is only fair to explain to those not completely *au fait* with anthropology that the Couvade Syndrome hasn't been seen in Europe for a few hundred thousand years.

And I'm afraid to say that, as far as I know, there are no plans to restore it – not just at present, anyway.

I

PREGNANCY

There are lots of interesting ways of making your wife pregnant and experimentation in this field is recommended. There are also lots of interesting ways of making someone else's wife pregnant, but this can cause unnecessary complications and, in general, should be avoided where possible.

For millennia, of course, men have been doing their damnedest to avoid getting their women pregnant. Drinking a mixture containing the pulverised testicles of a mule just before intercourse is said to do the trick, as is soaking the penis in vinegar or brine just before insertion, and if either of these methods appeal to you then by all means give them a go. Coitus interruptus is another traditional method of contraception although not one, we are informed in Genesis, that is much favoured by The Lord:

> And Judah said unto Onan
> Go in unto thy brother's wife
> and perform the duty of an husband's
> brother unto her, and raise up seed
> to thy brother.
> And Onan knew that the seed should not
> be his; and it came to pass, when he
> went into his brother's wife, that he spilled it on
> the ground, lest he should
> give seed to his brother.

For years this has been interpreted by the Church as an

act of self abuse on old Onan's part, but I would have thought that it was actually a pretty noble attempt by the poor blighter to use coitus interruptus to keep his brother's wife happy, do his duty, and yet avoid giving her an unwanted child. I would have thought ten out of ten for ingenuity, thoughtfulness and considerable self-restraint, but, alas for old Onan, The Lord didn't seem to see it this way, because the story ends thus:

> And the thing which he did was
> evil in the sight of The Lord; and He slew him.

It does seem amazing that, in this day and age, women can still get pregnant by mistake. You would have thought that, in an era of nuclear fission, star-wars and Sir Clive Sinclair, someone would have invented a device that was one hundred per cent efficient without giving you cancer. After hearing of at least three women who have become pregnant whilst using the coil I have rather reluctantly come to the conclusion that the only truly effective contraceptive device, apart from total abstinence, pulverised mules' testicles and spilling your seed all over the place is the condom, or French letter, and I'll tell you why.

A few months ago I was filming some interviews at a wine bar in Aldershot for a television documentary. While we were there groups of off-duty paratroopers came in and started drinking with the enthusiasm of those Ishmaelites in the Bible – probably chums of old Onan I wouldn't wonder – who had been wandering around the Sinai desert for a year or two without any provisions to speak of. After a time one of them suddenly shouted: 'Wings Parade, lads!' whereupon all thirty soldiers present leapt to attention, did an about-turn, pulled down their trousers and underpants and touched their toes, thus revealing one of the most revolting sights I have ever seen, to wit: thirty hairy bottoms sticking up in the air, each of them tattooed on the right buttock with the emblem of the Parachute Regiment. Apparently being tattooed on your buttock is absolute agony which, of course, is exactly why the paras do it.

What has all this to do with contraception, I hear you cry? Stick with it, I reply, all is about to be revealed.

Having covered up this hairy monstrosity and become once again decent in that respect at least, one of the paras then produced a packet of the above-mentioned French letters, took one out, pulled its neck wide open and pushed both his hands inside it, stretched it as wide as it would go and then, astonishingly, popped it over his head. He pulled it right down over his eyes to just below his nose so that his features were squashed and distorted like a bank-robber with some extremely tight tights over his face.

Then, to our absolute amazement, this lunatic proceeded to blow up the condom; this he did by inhaling through his mouth, which was free, and exhaling through his nose which was squashed flat beneath the thin, incredibly taut plastic. This then started to get bigger and bigger like a vast piece of bubble-gum. Gradually it took on the shape of some huge sausage-shaped balloon above his head, not getting much wider but simply taller and taller like a bishop's mitre until the obscene little tip on the top was scraping the ceiling. Quite extraordinary!

Eventually, after a round of rapturous applause, the soldier gave one final, almighty exhalation, whereupon the condom, with a deafening report, exploded. We all dived for cover and, when we realised precisely what had happened, we looked around the bar to see thin shreds of French letter hanging from the walls and ceiling.

This incredible episode convinced me of two things: a) any contraceptive that performs like that must be brilliantly well-made and therefore extremely reliable, and b) that the paras really are insane.

Anyway, assuming that you are aiming to spill your seed in just about the right sort of area then, providing you are a young, healthy and apparently fertile couple who enjoy frequent sex you would normally expect to conceive within six months and, if nowt has happened seed-wise after a year, it might be an idea to go along and have a word with your doctor. Women are most fertile as teenagers and the fertility of the average woman drops after the age of thirty-five, although a few women are able to conceive up to the age of fifty. Men, as old Abraham would have told you, can keep going until they drop. The last Sharifan Emperor of Morocco, Moulay Ishmail (1672–1727), known – for those interested in nicknames – as 'The Bloodthirsty', was reported to have fathered five hundred and twenty-five sons and three hundred and forty-two daughters by the age of thirty alone, and those were only the official offspring; after that they gave up counting. Family get-togethers in the Ishmail household must have been interesting. Standing-room only. Mind you, I suppose, when you consider that at each ejaculation a man produces up to 15 million sperm – that's more than the entire population of China – it is surprising we don't all produce a few cohorts more than we do.

* * *

The fertility of a couple has often been linked with the success of the harvest. The dance around the maypole, for example, was a traditional fertility dance and, in Indonesia, it is believed that the rice crop actually IS a pregnant woman. It is watched over and prayed for, and no loud noises or disturbances are allowed which might interfere with the pregnancy. When the time comes for harvesting, the news is kept secret from the rice and a special language is used when discussing the harvest in its 'hearing'.

Amongst the Bugandas of Central Africa, parents of twins are released from all normal village duties for a year and, instead, spend their time visiting childless couples in the district and performing sexual intercourse in front of them in the hope that their fertility will 'rub-off' onto the household in question, which I must say sounds a much better way of earning an honest crust than doing chores around the village. Again, if this idea appeals to you and you happen to know parents of twins, then by all means go ahead and ask them round to your place for tea.

I once had a brush with the perils of infertility myself.

I woke one morning to find my back teeth aching unbearably and the glands around my face blown up out of all proportion so that my neck totally disappeared and my head merged straight into my shoulders like a Michelin-tyre man, a particularly unfortunate affliction since I was in the midst of filming a television documentary at the time.

Dr Truscott, my GP, an attractive young woman whom I've always liked, immediately diagnosed mumps and told me to take a few days off work. The following week I returned to the office but gradually became aware, to my horror, that the pain and swelling had now moved down to what the Navy refers to as 'the lower deck'. Rather sheepishly I returned to my GP, quite an achievement in itself I might say since my left testicle, swollen to about four times its normal size, made it agony to walk. The only method of getting about at all was to keep my feet as wide apart as possible and hobble slowly forward with very small steps, which gave me the appearance of some poor soul racked by a terrible muscular disease and certainly caused a good deal of interest in the waiting-room, where just entering the room and lowering myself into a seat took about half an hour. When eventually it was my turn, I staggered in and was promptly instructed to remove my trousers.

For the first time I started to feel embarrassed. I carefully removed the trousers and stood there, feet about three yards apart, as though I was poised to begin an exhibition limbo dance.

'Pants, too, silly', said Dr Truscott and, having dropped these too, I felt like a schoolboy once again, lining up pantless for the cringe-making annual ballrot inspection when my form-master, an ex-army major with a bristling white moustache and a complete absence of any medical knowledge whatsoever would wander down the line, muttering 'Right, Wilkinson Minor, lift up the old bag of tricks and let's see what's brewing, eh? eh?' and then bend down double, peering through his extremely high-magnification pebble spectacles, examining us for evidence of goodness-knows-what frightful affliction.

I stood there awkwardly now, as Dr Truscott, an admiring whistle on her lips, began to feel my grossly oversized organ. Eventually, her hand still in position, she looked at me with a slightly maniacal glint in her eye.

'This is marvellous!'

'Marvellous?' I queried, wondering if I had heard her correctly.

'Marvellous! I'm very excited about this. I've always wanted to fit a Scrotum Stirrup and now here at last is my chance!'

I backed away as far as her tight grip would allow.

'Scrotum Stirrup?'

'Yes, yes', she continued, feverishly, as though announcing the launching of some divine crusade. 'It's a steel and leather contraption, just what's required to support this splendid thing!'

It sounded to me like some ghastly piece of mediaeval torture equipment and the thought of it strapped onto any part of me was quite appalling. This, then, was the moment to make a stand.

'No, no, not on your Nellie, no Scrotum Stirrup!' I said firmly.

'Oh, go on, please...'

'Out of the question!'

'Oh, I've never done one before...'

I refused to give way and eventually Dr Truscott, disappointed, arranged for me to drive straight away to the local hospital for a check-up. This, too, proved an ordeal. Because of my ongoing 'lower deck' scenario, it proved impossible for me to have my feet on both clutch and throttle at the same time, so when it came to changing gear I had to take my foot off the accelerator and swing my whole torso around so that my legs were wide enough apart to avoid offending the swollen organ in question, until my left foot could safely push down the clutch. Once or twice I had to break unexpectedly and the instinctive movement of my right foot meant that my legs were jerked together like a pair of nutcrackers and I was sent into spasms of pain, a sight which seemed to intrigue passers-by.

At the hospital I received immediate attention from the consultant – which just goes to prove my theory that, if you are young and worryingly ill you get first-class service from the NHS but, if you are old or permanently disabled, forget it – and after a thorough investigation with Ultrascan equipment to check that the blood flow through the lower deck was unimpaired I was told to go to bed for a fortnight and not move an inch, and to return in six weeks time to give a sperm sample to see whether the mumps had affected my fertility.

I didn't think anything of it at the time but, as the six-week deadline drew near, I began to worry about how the aforesaid sperm sample was actually taken. Anxious to offer reassurance, a colleague at work, who had just had a vasectomy, told me that, when he had been asked for a sample for counting, he had gone along to out-patients where a sister had marched up to him with a test-tube clasped in her hand and, in a resounding voice that had echoed around the entire building, told him to: 'Have a wank in that, love', pointing at a little cubicle on the other side of the room with a flimsy curtain pulled across, at which point the poor fellow wilted like a dying sunflower and nearly made a bolt for it.

At least that was his story and I found it so appalling that even the mere possibility that I would be shown into some grim little cubicle to do my duty, no doubt piled high with back copies of *Playboy* and *Men Only*, to emerge a few minutes later to be greeted by lascivious winks from the nurses and a chorus of 'We know what you've been doing' proved so mortifying that I couldn't sleep for days. I never did go back for that sample and a test-tube with my name written on it is probably gathering dust on some hospital shelf as you read this and since, my fertility seems relatively unimpaired to date, I think I shall keep it that way.

Since then, incidentally, I've discovered that, certainly in most hospitals these days, you are given a bottle which you can take home with you and which must be returned within a few hours of you filling it up, which sounds a bit more civilised.

From time to time since that problem a few years ago I have had a very slight ache in my lower deck and, when that happens, as instructed, I return promptly to Dr Truscott for a check-up, and we normally pass a pleasant ten minutes chatting about this and that whilst she fiddles with my balls to see if they are the shape which they are supposed to be and, to date, there have been no further complications.

Actually, to be honest, I've been tempted on a quiet evening when on my own to 'phone up and say there's an ache down there when there isn't, because Dr Truscott's conversation is so stimulating.

As a matter of fact, after one such visit, I arrived very late to work and the director I was filming with at the time asked me where I'd been. When I told him I'd been to see my doctor he didn't appear to believe me, saying: 'Oh come on, come clean, where have you been?'

'If you really want to know the truth, I'll tell you', I replied frostily. 'I've spent the morning having my balls played with by an attractive young blonde who I don't know at all well.'

He didn't ask again.

* * *

One evening you come home and the woman in your life is behaving in an extraordinary way. She takes your coat from you, kisses you affectionately and, with her arms wrapped around you, explains that dinner is already in the oven. Lovingly she runs her fingers through your hair and a drink is pushed into your hands.

Translated, this behaviour means she thinks she's pregnant. One of your 15 million sperm has excelled itself and, with the efficiency of an Exocet missile, has homed in perfectly on its target and hit the jackpot.

She's missed at least one period and has been to see the doc., who has examined her and taken a urine sample to confirm his suspicions. He is able to do this because your loved one has suddenly gone into producing a hormone called chorionic gonadotrophin in a big way. Lashings of it,

ONE OF YOUR 15,000,000 SPERM HAS EXCELLED ITSELF AND HAS HOMED IN PERFECTLY ON IT'S TARGET.

in fact. It started appearing as soon as the new embryo embedded itself in the lining of the uterus on the twenty-first day of the menstrual cycle and by the thirty-fifth day it is present in sufficiently large quantities to be detectable in the urine by means of a special test.

The news that it's all systems go may have some quite unexpected effects on you and your physiology. You may suddenly feel the urge to sing 'Hearts of Oak', dance a tango, stand on your head, vomit or throw yourself off the edge of a cliff. Personally, I remember my ear-lobes tingling violently.

Probably the most sensible course of action here is to knock back the drink that's just been pressed into your hand, and possibly have another. Then kiss her, long and passionately. Kiss her again. If your ear-lobes are still tingling kiss her again. Repeat the dose every few minutes. It is not possible to over-kiss at this stage.

The point about having babies is that they are considerate enough to give you nine months to get ready for them. You may indeed feel that this is much too long a time to wait and, should you feel like this, just be thankful that you are not a viviparous Alpine Black Salamander which, at high altitude, has a gestation period of over three years. Nine months, though, is quite a long time when you think about it, so postpone any drastic action, like throwing yourself off a cliff, and let time soften the blow. Keep up the kissing.

One of the first problems you will probably have to face is early morning sickness. This normally occurs following your first day at work after breaking the news to your colleagues. They will insist on taking you out and pouring as much alcohol down your gullet as physically possible. Early morning sickness will become apparent upon awakening next morning, but don't worry; it is a condition which you have experienced before, possibly on the morning of your marriage.

It is quite possible that the mother of your child is experiencing early morning sickness, too, although in the case of my wife it was early evening sickness, and here the remedy is much the same as for your own affliction, i.e. tough luck and just put up with it. Some women don't get nausea at all and others are laid out by it. I know someone who felt dreadfully ill all day every day for the first seven and a half months and, if you think you're having a bad time, then I'll give you her telephone number so that she can describe the details of her ordeal and I'll guarantee this will cheer you up. Apart from that, all you can usefully do is avoid suggesting a nice greasy bacon-and-sausage fry-up in the mornings, dish out instead bucketfuls of sympathy and dry biscuits, and reassure her that most early morning sickness ends in the third or fourth month of pregnancy.

It is possible that she'll get bizarre cravings to eat sawdust or pieces of coal but, in my experience, most of the bizarre cravings came from me. I took a great fancy to bread-and-butter pudding, which was very odd because I normally can't stand the stuff. I used to dream of mountains of bread-and-butter puddings. A study of expectant fathers in an American military camp found that they showed much more over-eating and gastro-intestinal illnesses than would have been expected. I did find, though, that my wife went into a series of emotional see-saws, one moment roaring with hysterical laughter over something I didn't find in the least amusing, and the next moment bursting into tears over some innocuous comment from a friend that was obviously not intended to hurt. Some women sink into deep depression and, even though having long wanted a baby, suddenly seem unsure about it. Don't take these moods seriously; just keep smiling and agreeing with her point of view like a grovelling peasant-labourer at the court of some tyrranical Chinese mandarin. Oh, and don't forget to keep up with the kissing.

As the pregnancy continues you'll also find she is spending more and more time either going to the lavatory or thinking about going to the lavatory. I read somewhere about a man who had been on a drinking spree with the actor Oliver Reed and they had ended up having a competition to see who could drink the most without urinating; if you can imagine that then you are well placed to understand how a woman must feel with a bulging great baby constantly sitting on her bladder. Making jokes about her preoccupation will go down extremely badly, especially in company, so – as with the fatigue she will increasingly begin to feel as the pregnancy wears on – take it for granted and play everything down. Keep kissing her.

During pregnancy, you may often find yourself asking the question: 'How about sex?' This is a good question to put to your partner because, despite one's natural inhibitions, you would need to have an organ the size of a garden hose to actually do your baby any damage during intercourse. In fact, sex during pregnancy can be marvellous. For a start, the gradual changing of her shape will mean that you'll need to consider a whole range of imaginative positions for intercourse which you had never even dreamed of before. Secondly, during pregnancy, the woman in your life will undoubtedly look ravishingly attractive. All those hormones whizzing around inside her will make her hair gleam, skin glow and eyes sparkle like never before. Sometimes all the fast-moving hormones mean that a woman's sexual appetite actually increases during pregnancy. Some men, too, find pregnant women inherently sexually exciting. A colleague of mine once confessed that he had sexual fantasies about pregnant women, preferably, he said, pregnant women who were extremely muscular and were dressed only in VERY tight-fitting leotards. So far, he explained, he hadn't had much luck in this direction.

Thanks to the suspension of the menstrual cycle you will also be able to have sex as frequently as you like with no restrictions whatsoever. And don't forget that even the suggestion of sex shows that you still find your partner very attractive, a fact which she, thanks to her increasingly rotund silhouette, will probably worry about a good deal more than you may think.

But there is one other big advantage which sex during pregnancy has over sex at all other times in your life. It is something which many couples find a wonderful release, a weight off the shoulders, an unshackling of a chain which, before and after, may even have dominated their thoughts on making love, and even dominated the very way they made love.

Contraception has suddenly become a thing of the past. Whatever else you may be worrying about, you certainly need have no fears now about making her pregnant.

And that must be worth another kiss.

2

PREPARATIONS

One recent study showed that men whose wives were pregnant were more likely to be suffering from depression and mental upset, and were more likely to be arrested for sexually-deviant offences, such as exhibitionism.

It doesn't surprise me in the least.

For a start, there is suddenly another human being in your life which is demanding a great deal of your time and attention, and I'm not talking about the baby; I mean the bank manager. When you sit down to consider the long-term financial implications of having a baby it is not surprising that you may feel like one of those cartoon characters with his hair standing on end who has suddenly found himself holding a bomb that's about to explode.

Curiously, when a woman becomes pregnant, money no longer holds any value for her whatsoever. For example, the flat or house where you may have been living in spacious luxury for years will suddenly no longer be big enough. Even if you happen to live in Buckingham Palace you will be constantly reminded that the place simply doesn't have enough rooms and, at the same time, you will suddenly find estate agent's details hidden under cushions around the house.

You are told that not only is it quite amazing that you've been managing to live in such a tiny place for so long, but all of a sudden isn't it just incredible that you haven't redecorated recently? I mean have you noticed how tatty and dirty everything looks? Of course the baby's room must be done at once and, whilst you're at it, you may as well do the outside as well.

You will need a crib, and obviously you don't want a second-hand one, and a cot. You will need a pram and a pushchair, a baby bath and feeding chair. You will need a ton or two of ordinary nappies and a juggernaut's worth of disposables; vests and plastic pants, babygros and nightdresses, cardigans, shawls, bootees, helmets and mittens. Upstairs you will have to fit a completely new set of cupboards and shelves in bedrooms and bathrooms, and downstairs the kitchen will have to be re-equipped from scratch, don't you think, it makes sense while we're about it, doesn't it? Clearly this is the best time to entirely re-design the garden to take into account dangerous steps, lack of gates, and the fact that there is nowhere suitable for the sandpit and swing. The car needs new seat belts fitted in the back but, since the boot's too small to hold the pram and pushchair together anyway, you might just as well get a new one – mightn't you?

When you point out that all this, combined with a new life-insurance policy and the loss of income brought about by the fact that, of course, she is giving up work to have the baby, might, just conceivably, result in the teeniest little overdraft, you will be given a look of total astonishment. The following conversation will then take place:

'It's just I'm not sure we can afford it all at once, darling.'

'So what?'

Quite short, as conversations go, I'll admit but, after a long pause, the exchange will resume, almost certainly as follows:

'It's just that with our overdraft . . .'

'Don't you CARE about your baby?'

GARDEN FURNITURE
CLIMB FRAME
LOFT CONVERSION KIT
DIY STORES
NAPPIES
MATT VYNIL
GLOSS
UNDER COAT
BILL
NAPPIES
NAPPIES
NAPPIES

It's just around this point in your life that A Truth will suddenly become apparent. Not only are you no longer the only person in her life; the chances are that, when it comes to the actual details of her batting order, you may well find yourself going in at Number 2. This is presumably why some fathers, feeling a certain lack of attention, suddenly feel the urge to go around the place exposing themselves.

What will also become apparent, but not necessarily at the same time, is that she is now not the only person in YOUR life either, and that we should have the basis for an equilateral triangle. And let's just say that, with luck, the square of the hypotenuse should in time turn out to be roughly opposite to the sum of the opposite two angles.

If things get too out of hand you can always diffuse some of the tension by raising the subject of names for the baby. I have worked out that most couples waiting for a baby to arrive spend between ninety-eight point six and ninety-nine point eight of their waking hours discussing names. It is without any doubt one of the world's most boring pastimes. But it is soothing. It calms troubled waters. It reassures. And it gives your ticket to immortality some kind of identity, which may at least make your negotiations with the bank manager seem a little more worthwhile.

Recently a couple called John and Margret Nelson, who live in Chesterfield, Derbyshire, had a baby daughter and, after much deliberation, they gave her the following first names:

Tracy Mariclaire Lisa Tammy Samantha Christine Alexandra Candy Bonnie Ursula Zoe Nichola Patricia Lynda Kate Jean Sandra Karren Julie Jane Elizabeth Felicity Gabriella Jackie Corina Constance Arabella Clara Honor Geraldine Fiona Erika Fillipa Anabel Elsie Amanda Cheryl Alanna Louisa Angie Beth Crystal Dawn Debbie Eileen Grace Susan Rebecca Valerie Kay Lena Margaret Anna

Amy Carol Bella Avril Ava Audry Andrea Daphne Donna Cynthia Cassie Christabel Vivien Wendy Moira Jennifer Abbie Adelaide Carrissa.

Carla Anna Astrid Barbara Charissa Catalina Bonny Dee Hazel Iris Anthea Clarinda Bernadette Cara Alison Carrie Angela Beryl Caroline Emma Dana Vanessa Zara Violet Lynn Maggie Pamela Rosemary Ruth Cathlene Alexandrina Annette Hilary Diana Angelina Carrinna Victoria Sara Mandy Annabella Beverley Bridget Cecilia Catherine Brenda Jessica Isobella Delilah Camila Candice Helen Connie Charmaine Dorothy Melinda Nancy Mariam Vicki Selina Miriam Norma Pauline Toni Penny Shari Zsa-Zsa Queenie.

When asked why he had picked so many first names, the above's father replied, with eminent logic, I thought: 'Because we liked them'. I think most of the nation's returning officers would agree with me in hoping she never stands for Parliament.

Whilst we are on the subject, you will be fascinated to learn that Britain's longest-ever surname belonged to a gentleman called Major Leone Sextus Denys Oswolf Fraudati Filius Tollemache-Tollemache-de Orellana-Plantagenet-Tollemache-Tollemache. Unfortunately, Major Leone Sextus Denys Oswolf Fraudati Filius Tollemache-Tollemache-de Orellana-Plantagenet-Tollemache-Tollemache made the cardinal error of dying of pneumonia in 1917 without having any children.

Mind you, you can guarantee that whatever name you do eventually choose, your child will grow to hate it. My brother announced at the age of six he no longer wished to be referred to by the name given to him by my parents, Roger, but that in future he would only answer to the name Perseus. He was quite serious about it, too; for months my poor mother had to creep about the garden calling out, as softly as she could: 'Perseus! Perseus! Lunch is ready'! in the constant fear that the neighbours would hear.

* * *

From time to time, you may just find yourself with a moment or two to spare in which you may like to consider your position and ponder the cataclysmic upheaval that lies, like some alpine precipice, a few feet in front of you. To say that life will never be the same again is the kind of understatement which will have anyone who already has children falling around the aisles with laughter. The changes in your personality and that of the mother of your child will be so dramatic that you will almost certainly actually become different people – the shadowy memories of your life without children, which may fleetingly haunt you every now and then, will read like the biography of a total stranger.

How far is it possible to predict these changes? Just how big an impact will the infant preparing to burst forth make on your lives? Is your individuality now under threat? Which corner of the new triangular relationship of which you are now just one part will have the greatest pull? And why is it that anything remotely connected with the subject of psychology always has to be in the form of a question?

In an effort to find some answers I made the mistake of turning to Freud. Well, dammit, he was supposed to be the greatest psycho-analyst of his time, wasn't he? Didn't he devote his life to the study of the human mind and of human relationships, particularly in the family? Well, did he or didn't he?

Quite a guy, old Freud. I picked up one of his books and, flicking it open somewhere in the middle, I started to read.

THE SHADOWY MEMORIES OF YOUR LIFE WITHOUT CHILDREN WILL READ LIKE A BIOGRAPHY OF A TOTAL STRANGER.

One day a young woman patient came to Freud with a dream she wished him to interpret. Reasonable enough, of course; interpreting people's dreams was how the old fellow paid the mortgage. This was the dream:

> I was walking in the street in the summer, wearing a straw hat of peculiar shape; its middle-piece bent upwards and its side-pieces hung downwards in such a way that one side was lower than the other. I was cheerful and in a self-confident frame of mind; and, as I passed a group of young officers, I thought: 'None of you can do me any harm'!

That's it.

Now, everyone enjoys having a stab at interpreting other people's dreams, don't they? Oh, I wouldn't wonder that you already know the answer to this one. Pretty straightforward, I know. Forgive me if it's been too easy for you.

At first, though, I have to admit I was a bit puzzled. I mean, she must have looked a bit of a prat wandering around in a hat like that. Where on earth did she get it from? And anyway, is that all that happened? Sounded like a pretty boring dream to me.

Freud, of course, found it fascinating. He came straight out with his interpretation without the slightest hesitation and, just in case you haven't been able to work it out for yourself, this is the gist of what he said: the hat, of course, represented the male genital organ, with the bit sticking up the penis and the bits hanging down, one lower than the other, the testes and the reason she spoke like that to the young officers was that, as she had a husband with such fine genitals, there was no need for her to be afraid of them; no need, that is, for her to wish for anything from them.

Obvious, isn't it? I mean, of course a young woman walking around with a hat which looks like a penis on her head would think that, wouldn't she? As a matter of fact I admire her for her courage. I wouldn't be seen dead in a hat that looks like a penis and I can tell you that, if I had to wear a hat like that, I wouldn't hang around casting cheerful and self-confident looks at anyone, particularly soldiers.

It's a pity Freud wasn't around long enough to have had the chance to take along his notebook to Ladies' Day at Ascot.

As you'd expect, the old boy had a good deal to say about the relationship between father/mother/son/daughter. Oh yes, a good bit actually. In a nutshell, this is the position and, as impending paternity draws closer, it is your duty to absorb the following.

Briefly, an examination of our dreams shows beyond doubt that, if you have a daughter, she will fall in love with you and, sexually jealous of her mother, will wish her dead so that she can sleep with you; if you have a son, he will fall in love with his mother and, sexually jealous of you, will wish you dead so that he can sleep with her.

O.K.?

And good luck.

* * *

Bank manager willing, it's also extremely important at this stage to do a few of the things you may never have the chance to do again, at least for a few years. For example, deciding to catch the next plane to Honolulu so that you can eat raw oysters on the beach at sunrise is not something which you will have the opportunity to do every weekend when the baby's arrived. Go to the theatre, throw an all-night party, have a weekend away with friends. Live dangerously. You will have plenty of time over the next quarter of a decade to catch up on reading *The Forsyte Saga*.

What really surprised me was the way everyone, EVERYONE is interested in a new baby.

For example, we had one very humiliating false alarm when my wife Mo was quite convinced that The Moment Had Finally Come. We rushed out to the car, bearing huge brown suitcases full of provisions and clothes that we had prepared weeks ago, and had been lying by the front door in readiness and been a bloody nuisance ever since. We lived in a little cul-de-sac at the time, when all comings and goings were observed with scrupulous reliability and tremendous interest by ladies peering out of the corners of net curtains. On this occasion, the size of Mo's girth and the selection of large brown suitcases produced more than the usual interest.

When we got to the hospital, however, they all fell about with laughter and told us to go home. The arrival back at the cul-de-sac, and the subsequent unloading of the aforesaid large brown suitcases with Mo's girth still at its former size, meant that net curtains that hadn't seen the light of day for years were now going up and down like yo-yos.

When quizzed casually about it by desperately inquisitive neighbours later, I explained that we had merely been exchanging our new set of suitcases which turned out to have faulty locks.

'Shop was only too happy to replace them,' I said, with a smile.

'Oh, we all thought you had had a false alarm.'

'False alarm? What on earth do you mean?'

'Well, the baby . . .'

'Oh Good Lord no! What a thought!' etc. etc.

When our baby did decide to start arriving, several days later, I was in the depths of the New Forest, interviewing a senior oil executive about his plans to drill for oil in the middle of one of the most beautiful areas of oak woodland in the country. I had been quite aggressive in my questions, vigorously putting forward the arguments of local conservationists that drilling could ruin the Forest for ever.

The man wasn't pleased with me; he had not performed well and, when we had finished, his face had clouded over with the colour of a brewing thunderstorm and, complaining bitterly that I had given him a hard time, he wandered off back to his little team of advisors and cronies standing a few feet away muttering about 'bloody media people'.

Just then my car's radio-telephone, an item with which most television reporters are equipped when out on location, suddenly burst into life and I received the message that Mo was on her way to hospital.

'Look, I'm sorry', I said to the group of scowling oilmen. 'I'm afraid I'm going to have to go now, my wife's having a baby'.

The word 'baby' had a remarkable effect. I shall never forget it. The senior man, who moments before had been kicking the earth with his boot and glaring at me, suddenly gave a massive beaming grin, which seemed to split his face from ear to ear, exposing a set of gleaming, perfect-white teeth which caught the early morning sunlight and dazzled me with their brilliance. Then the fellow slapped me between the shoulder blades with such force that I nearly toppled forward. After this he gave a little hop and a skip, dancing back to his colleagues singing 'A baby! A baby!' whilst the rest of them queued up to wring my hand.

They were still at it as I drove away through the Forest, still skipping around each other beneath the ancient oaks crying 'A baby! A baby!' like a group of drunken morris-dancers.

It has that effect on some people.

3

THE BIRTH

It never ceases to amaze me how medical opinion can change so dramatically at the mere drop of a hat.

A few years ago, for example, if you burned your finger then positively the last thing you should ever EVER do is put the offending appendage under the tap, despite the fact that your common sense tells you that this has got to be the best way of cooling it down. Then, overnight, and after a few hundred million years of man's existence, the medical profession suddenly makes the following announcement: 'Sorry, folks, we've made a bit of a cock-up here, what we really meant was that the very FIRST thing you should do when you burn your finger is to put it straight under the tap. Best thing for it. Cools it down, you see.'

So it seems with most aspects of childbirth. When my mother gave birth to me just over thirty years ago, my father, despite the fact he was actually a doctor, was told that fathers were not allowed within several miles of the labour ward for fear that they would 'get in the way' or, to give it its official medical description, 'be a bloody nuisance'. Even more extraordinary was that my mother, upon arrival at the hospital and well into the first stage of labour, was greeted by a very large Matron, a lady who could have done passably well in the auditions for Hattie Jacques' role in the *Carry On* movies, who insisted that she sit down to a three-

FATHERS WERE NOT ALLOWED WITHIN SEVERAL MILES OF THE LABOUR WARD.

course meal, consisting of a roast and two veg, jam roly-poly and cheese and biscuits, arguing that it didn't do you any good to give birth on an empty stomach. My poor mother pointed out that at this moment she just didn't feel too hungry but the Matron said that she must remain at the table until all the plates were clean and was so fearsome about it that my mother, in no mood for a fight, capitulated, promptly bringing the entire meal back up a few minutes afterwards, although, unfortunately, Matron had wisely moved a few steps just out of range at the time.

These days, naturally, you are expected to do precisely the opposite.

Whether you do or do not attend the birth of your child is something you must decide for yourself and, despite any conclusions you may draw from the pages that follow, let me make it clear now that I am very glad indeed I was there at the births of both my children. It is a most extraordinary event and, for most men, one of the most memorable of their lives, but if you or your partner feel strongly that you shouldn't be there, don't feel pressurised into going. Recently I heard about a couple from Birmingham, called Lionel and Irene Felton who, having already had ten boys, found an eleventh child was on the way. Now at the births of Lionel Junior, now seventeen, Robin (sixteen), Gary (fourteen), Neil (thirteen), Michael (twelve), Paul (eleven), Neville (six), Shaun (five), Clint (three) and Martin (two), Mrs Felton had insisted on her husband Lionel not being present. This time, however, she went agin' her instinct and gave the all-clear for him to hove-to. Two remarkable things happened. The first was that, instead of having a girl, as she had hoped, Mrs Felton produced an eleventh boy, against odds of 2047 to 1. The second was that Mr Felton, observing the birth of another human being for the first time ever was appalled and horrified by what he saw. 'I wish I had not been there', the poor man said afterwards. 'I did not like it one bit. I never appreciated what women had to go through.' And then, as a final afterthought, Mr Felton added: 'We shall not be having any more children.'

Either way, you will need to be at the hospital and for this you must be well-prepared. If you are very keen, you can pack up a suitcase beforehand to be grabbed at a moment's notice; make sure it includes the following:

1. A vast box of tissues.
2. Another vast box of tissues.
3. An extremely long novel, preferably one with a plot that doesn't rely on too many difficult births.
4. A big cushion to protect your backside from the ravages that will be caused by hour after hour of ancient hospital chairs.
5. Smelling-salts, to be handed to the trainee midwife when you – or she – pass out.
6. More tissues.
7. A hip-flask filled with vodka, a spirit which can't be detected on your breath. For some inexplicable reason they don't have bars in most hospitals – at least, not unless you happen to be a member of staff.
8. A Fortnum and Mason food-hamper.

This last item is quite essential. Your stint in hospital may last for an extremely long time and whilst most maternity hospitals do quite well in feeding staff, babies and mothers – in that order – fathers are sadly absent from any of the catering arrangements. I can tell you that a slice of smoked salmon washed down with the odd stuffed olive can be most restorative, even at moments of crisis.

And if you think I'm joking about all this let me remind you that the first stage of labour in a first pregnancy will probably last about fifteen hours. During this time the neck of the uterus will gradually be opening wide enough to allow your baby to begin its journey to the outside world. When labour begins, the contractions will last less than half a minute and come every fifteen minutes or so, but don't rush off to hospital until the contractions are lasting for forty-five seconds. Don't panic about this – you will probably have an absolute age to wait before anything important happens, and most couples – like us – find that, nine times out of ten, they arrive much too early rather than too late.

If, in a million to one chance, you find that the recurrent new father's nightmare of breaking down on the way to hospital in the middle of a dark country lane miles from the nearest habitation and having to deliver the baby yourself is actually happening, then make sure you have this book with you. There is an emergency procedure which it is vital for you to follow and, to make sure that this procedure stands out and can be found easily, I have printed it in capitals. Take a good look at it now as well, and make sure you remember every detail, just in case you forget to have this book with you.

This is it:

1. WISH YOURSELF GOOD LUCK.
2. DO NOTHING (first stage of labour).
3. DO NOTHING (second stage of labour).

OK? Do you think you can manage that? I know it is asking a lot but, if you feel lacking in confidence, then try rehearsing each item on the list in the privacy of your own home.

Right, so now you going to try to convince me that you are still stuck in the car after sixteen hours and no one has passed you on that lonesome road to offer help? You expect me to believe that? All right, so for the sake of assuaging the nightmare, this is what you should do if you are still stranded after the second stage of labour:

4. DO NOTHING. (Assuming its a normal birth, trying to help pull the baby, cord or placenta can only do damage.)
5. ONCE THE BABY IS BORN, DO NOTHING. (Trying to cut or tie the cord before the placenta emerges can only do damage.)
6. FINALLY, DO NOTHING.
7. OH, ALL RIGHT, IF YOU MUST DO SOMETHING, KEEP THE BABY WARM.
8. WAIT FOR PASSING TRACTOR.

Strictly the cord should be cut about ten minutes after your baby has been born and, if by an amazing coincidence you happen to have some sterilised string and scissors in your glove compartment (don't we all?), then tie the string around the cord as tightly as you can in two places about an inch apart at a distance of about six inches from your baby's navel; put two extra knots either side of the first two and cut between the two sets of ties. Then do nothing again. If by some chance the placenta still hasn't arrived of its own accord, you have about an hour to get help. If you don't have sterilised scissors and string with you, then do nothing. Baby and mother can survive quite comfortably for quite a few hours.

When Mo and I were finally admitted to hospital we sat around for what seemed like several days trying to do the crossword and reading Reginald Bosanquet's autobiography which I remember only because it is called *Let's Get Through Wednesday* which, since it was a Wednesday, seemed a good choice. After several shift changes, during which we saw whole teams of midwives come and go, a man in a white coat arrived, bearing a long thin piece of white plastic with its end sharpened like a quill pen which, without so much as a by-your-leave, he proceeded to shove up Mo in a most undignified way. This, I was just about able to establish later, was an attempt to 'break the waters', i.e. rupture the bag of membranes surrounding the baby and thus get the whole procedure under starter's orders. Incidentally, if the waters break while you are still at home then you should go to hospital immediately, regardless of whether contractions appear to have started or not.

After the man in the white coat had done his duty, what seemed like another couple of days passed. Eventually, a lady in a white coat suggested that I should help Mo walk up and down the corridor in the hope that all the pelvic motion which walking involves, combined with the pull of gravity, might give our baby the hint that it was time to be on the move. Poor Mo look worried.

'It seems to be taking a very long time. Do you think everything's all right?' she asked nervously.

'Oh yes, indeedy-doody, my dear', I replied, trying to sound as though I earned a living from delivering babies. 'Everything's going to be just tickety-boo, don't worry about an itsy-witsy thing'. Why I suddenly started talking like a demented three-year-old I shall never know, but I suppose it was an attempt to sound casual and relaxed. Much later, Mo said my behaviour at this stage alarmed her much more than any fears about the birth.

Just at that moment a scream the like of which I have never heard before or since rang out down the corridor; if I had hairs on the back of my neck this would have been the moment for them to leap to attention. It was a positively blood-curdling scream coming from one of the delivery-rooms and it was followed by some terrible, tortured gasps and then another ghastly werewolf-like howl, ending with the words: 'Jesus Christ! I want to die! Please let me die!'

For a moment Mo and I look at each other in silence.

'Come along', I muttered dryly, forcing a fixed smile

AAAAAGH! UGH! UGH! I WANT TO DIE. PLEASE LET ME DIE.!!
WAITING ROOM

onto my pale and drawn face. 'Let's see if we can finish the crossword'.

* * *

After a time Mo seemed to become more and more agitated, lying on the bed on her side, breathing rapidly with eyes revolving like the flashing lights on a pinball machine, a condition which worried me but delighted the midwives, who came over from time to time smiling happily and muttering 'Good, good', and a few hours later 'Excellent, excellent'. I didn't have to be Sherlock Holmes to realise that by this time, as she writhed in agony on the bed beside me, Mo appeared to have lost the track of *Let's Get Through Wednesday* completely. I can tell you it's a pretty lonely experience sitting in a huge labour ward, with the woman you love in appalling discomfort beside you, reading out Reginald Bosanquet's biography aloud with no one taking the slightest notice, but there you are.

After another few hours Mo suddenly grabbed one of my hands and guided it down to the small of her back where, by a series of grunting commands, I realised she was expecting me to rub her. This I obediently did and, for a moment or two, it seemed to give some relief, although it was quite tiring on my arm and I soon started to slow up a little, whereupon Mo started beating me. I speeded up the old rubbing again and this seemed to soothe the fevered brow for a few more minutes but my arm was soon aching so much I had to slow down again. This time Mo turned and began flailing me with both her arms about my head and shoulders, which was quite painful. A moment or two later I was forced to scratch my nose and immediately violent blows rained down all over my upper torso. This was the moment, I decided rather reluctantly, to abandon Reginald Bosanquet, who by this time I had begun to get to know pretty well, but even alternating hands for the endless task of rubbing didn't prevent further severe beatings every time I paused for even a split second. By the time Mo was at last shipped off to the delivery-room I was black and blue all over, and limping badly too, where Mo had caught my upper thigh with a superb left cut. When, a long time later, I phoned up my mother-in-law to tell her the baby had eventually been born and she asked how everything had gone I said fine, although my right shoulder and neck still seemed very sore. She didn't seem in the least sympathetic.

Things still seemed to be taking an eternity so one of the midwives, addressing me for the first time ever, suggested I take a break from the event for ten minutes or so and, with a degree of relief it must be said, I agreed and limped down to the waiting-room beside the labour ward where I came across a doctor fully dressed in blood-stained surgical gown, boots, hat and face-mask which he had pushed up over his nose so he could puff away at a large cigar. It was rather like a scene from *M.A.S.H.* and, although he looked like some refugee consultant from a particularly mucky Caesarean operation, he seemed very friendly.

'Evenin', how's it going then mate?' he asked me kindly.

'Well', I said, only too glad of the opportunity to talk to another rational human being. 'My wife is very agitated and excited and seems to be hitting me rather a lot. Is this normal?'

His reply surprised me.

'Gawd knows, me old cocker. I've forgotten everything I once knew about this lark.' And with this he went off, stumbling slightly, towards his front-line operating theatre whilst I wondered whether it was too late for Mo and I to make a bolt for it.

It was only later, when the midwife handed me a surgical gown that I realised that, far from being a doctor, the chap I'd met was simply another poor sod like me. Poor sod.

If you don't intend to witness the birth then it's on the way from the labour ward to the delivery-room that you part company with your loved one. If you press on then in the delivery-room you will be expected to do a few menial tasks which are designed to make you believe you are doing something useful, which I suppose they do. I was given a sponge, for example, and was just about to wipe my own worried brow with it when the midwife pointed out it was intended for my wife. Mo was also dying of thirst but, because of the problems of filling up the old bladder at such a critical moment, she was only allowed ice-cubes to suck, and I fed her these like a conveyor belt. In fact the midwives had been jumping up and down for some time in an effort to encourage poor Mo to spend a penny but, probably for the first time in her life, Mo found herself unable to perform satisfactorily; to add extra persuasion to their argument they then turned on all the taps in the delivery room in the hope that the sound of running water splashing all over the place might produce results which, whilst having not the slightest effect on Mo, had me scurrying to the 'Gents' like one demented.

By now Mo had been in labour a very long time and, because she seemed to be a little distressed, they gave her a shot of pethidine. This is a reasonably mild pain-killer which takes about ten minutes to act and will last several hours. It doesn't numb the mother completely, which isn't what most mothers want anyway, but it does take the edge off the pain and we'd already decided beforehand that if Mo felt she needed it then she should take it. Some parents decide to do without any drugs at all and, if this is so in your case, then tell the medical staff about your decision before you get into the delivery-room. What concerns them, of course, is that pain-killers interfere with natural childbirth but we felt that, although pethidine does slightly depress the baby's respiration, the benefits in terms of relaxing Mo and reducing the length of labour – in itself beneficial to the health of the baby – outweighed this. A rather more dramatic form of pain-killer is the epidural, which is administered *via* a catheter inserted into the base of the spinal cord, actually between the bones of the spinal column, which remains in position throughout the birth. This gets rid of all pain but it can also mean the mother loses that powerful urge to push, and it can mean a drop in blood pressure. That, combined with the delicacy with which the catheter has to be inserted, means the epidural is only suggested if it is strictly necessary. On top of that, there will be that bottle of nitrous oxide plus mask that can be used for short bursts of pain relief or relaxation which, as you may remember, I can vouch for with some authority (see Introduction).

Incidentally, whatever your feelings about the use of drugs in the delivery-room – or anywhere else for that – you must at least give the British Pharmaceutical Industry credit for perseverance in its determination to push back the frontiers of science. A couple of weeks ago I met a friend of mine who, amongst other things, earns a living from writing drug advertisements for use in medical videos for doctors. He looked a bit down in the dumps so I asked what was the matter.

'I've got to write an advert for a new drug that's just come out to combat severe flatulence', he informed me gloomily.

'You mean it stops people farting?' I asked helpfully and, I might add, with a certain degree of interest in his reply.

'No, no', he muttered. 'I wish it was as simple as that. No, what it does is make 'em smell nice. Adds a kind of peppermint fragrance. Jolly good idea for those with a farting problem, I'll admit, but a bastard of an idea to get across in a television commercial.'

I could see his point.

Anyway, getting back to this having-babies-bit, there is one point which you really do need to know and which, naturally enough, no one actually gets round to telling you beforehand, and it's this: if there's any kind of a problem with the birth of your baby you will be asked to leave the room. I wish I had known this when a doctor suddenly appeared waving a pair of glistening steel scissors like the High Priest of some bizarre religious sect and started to slice open a rather important area of Mo's anatomy with the enthusiasm of a small boy cutting out the free cardboard racing-car on the back of a cornflake packet. I eventually discovered that what he was doing was making a cut at the base of the vagina, about an inch long, to make a rather bigger escape route for the baby. The medical profession, of course, bashful about this, as in so many cases, is embarrassed to call it a vaginal cut and instead calls it an episiotomy, which, like most of their language, is totally meaningless to everyone except the chosen few. And I can tell you, the sight of a stranger with steel scissors, ravaging a part of my wife which I hold particularly dear, distracted me so much that I found I was stuffing about three ice-cubes into Mo's mouth at once. The point about this vaginal cut – sorry, episiotomy – is that it not only makes delivery easier, but it is also considerably less awkward to repair, i.e. stitch up, than a tear that may happen anyway; it may also mean that the piece of skin and muscle immediately between the vagina and anus – sorry, the perineum – isn't badly stretched, and I'm told a stretched perineum can lead to greater problems in later life when, like the foundations of a house after a severe drought, it causes subsidence to all the gynaecological

THE DOCTOR SUDDENLY APPEARED WAVING
A PAIR OF GLISTENING STEEL SCISSORS.

equipment which rests above it.

Suddenly I could see a little circle of hair about the size of an old half-crown moving slowly down toward the outside world. It seemed to be moving very slowly indeed, actually, and I suppose because of the excitement and effects of the nitrous oxide, I assumed that this was the head of my baby in its entirety, which looked at logically in the clear, nitrous-oxide-free air of day is quite absurd because it would have meant Tom being born with a head the size of a ping-pong ball. His head, when, with a rush, it burst out of captivity, was in fact a perfectly normal size but to me, at that moment, it seemed quite huge; much, much too big to ever have grown inside Mo and certainly too big to have made that slow journey through such a narrow tunnel. The sight of this extraordinary-looking creature, brown with a purplish tinge, and with a head thirty times the size of the average ping-pong ball was such a shock that I burst into tears. Seeing your own baby for the first time is an extraordinary moment. I suppose partly it is surprise – surprise that the baby isn't some hypothetical, inanimate object as it has been before, but really alive, with a perceivable identity, face, personality all of its own; and surprise, too, that the baby is never anything like you may have imagined it to be. I found it a profound moment.

After a minute or two of admiration we wiped away the tears and found ourselves quickly plunged back into the maze of physiological minutiae. The umbilical cord was cut, Tom was given a quick wipe and thrust into Mo's arms, then mine, when I looked at him thinking: 'Who on earth are you?' and he looked at me thinking: 'Who on earth are YOU?' The placenta made its appearance, slightly less dramatically than Tom's arrival, and then poor Mo, as if she hadn't suffered enough, had to have her episiotomy sewn up, a process she found far more painful than having the baby and considerably more ignominious.

A generation ago when our parents were having us, the prospect of a woman being given a Caesarean section could cause a great deal of fear and worry but, since the early sixties, it has become very safe indeed and now accounts for about six per cent of all deliveries. The other day I met a doctor and asked him what were some of the reasons that may prompt a Caesarean and, with typical helpfulness, he said: 'Oh, placenta praevia, pelvic fibroids, eclampsia, even pre-eclampsia, disproportion, accidental antepartum haemorrhage, that kind of thing – clear now?' This conflicted slightly with the reasons I'd heard from one experienced father who claimed that Caesareans were often administratively convenient, particularly if the gynaecologist concerned felt that the birth of your child by vaginal delivery might mean he would miss watching the final round of the US Masters Golf Championships on television. In fact, Caesareans are only ever given in order to reduce the risks posed by the alternative, and these might include things like your baby gradually being starved of oxygen as labour continues; your baby lying in the uterus in totally the wrong position for delivery, such as horizontally instead of head first; or severe bleeding behind or around the placenta.

The other point about the Caesarean is that it gets everything over very quickly indeed, a tremendous benefit under normal circumstances given the solidity of most hospital chairs but particularly if mother or child is in distress. The operation is often completed within three-quarters of an hour, although I met another doctor recently (I seem to know a lot of doctors) who gave me the most amazing details about the work he did a few years ago in a remote emergency bush hospital in the Transkei in South Africa. He was often forced to carry out Caesareans without anaesthetic, either because the women, often having walked hundreds of miles to get to him, were too far gone, or they objected to anaesthetics on principle, or often simply because there was no anaesthetist on hand. So instead of all that he used a witch-doctor, who would come into the operating theatre in full regalia and dance about mumbling this and that until, through growing excitement and acute hyperventilation, the mother would go into a short trance and the w.-doctor would give a wink saying 'Fire away, doc.!' and this poor guy had about five minutes flat to whip the baby out.

Interesting fella, actually; he used to carry out circumcisions in the same way. When he arrived, he was horrified to hear that, when the young males in the local tribes reached about fourteen or fifteen years of age, they were taken out into the bush and given an initiation ceremony by the w.-doctor which often lasted several days and would include quite a few sensible lessons in self-defence, hunting, the facts of life and all the other knowledge required to convert them from boys to men. The ceremony climaxed with circumcision, in which all the boys were lined up and had their foreskins sliced off by the w.-doctor using nothing more than a sharp stone – I know, it's painful just to think about it – and all this, I might add, without crying out or even wincing. Many of them, of course, suffered terrible ravages and infections to this important area of their anatomy and when the doctor arrived fresh-faced from Merry England and heard about all this he nearly had a fit. What made things worse was that the hospital was staffed by nuns who refused even to discuss the subject, so eventually our doc. suggested a compromise: If you must do all this without anaesthetics, use the w.-doctor to put the boys into a trance and at least let me use my experience plus a very sharp and clean scalpel to do the rest – and that's just what he did. The nuns never knew a thing about it. He reckons he can carry out a circumcision faster than any other doctor around –

between twenty or thirty seconds a piece – and if you ever need a circumcision in a hurry I will gladly pass on his address.

Well, having been through the rigours of Tom's birth without the need for witch-doctors, Caesareans, or even circumcisions, but with a great deal of nerves, terror and finally delight, I felt very well prepared indeed for the birth of our second child, a daughter Alex, seventeen months later. I knew now precisely what to expect, and hamper, hip-flask and buttock-protective cushion had long since been packed ready and waiting. I even wore extra vests and jumpers to protect me from hour after hour of Mo's beatings.

But then that's Sod's Law, isn't it? This time everything was different; Alex was born within an hour of us arriving at hospital, the midwife didn't have time to offer Mo pethidine and I didn't even have time to open Chapter 1 of Sandy Gall's autobiography *Don't Worry About The Money Now*.

4

POST-OPERATIVE SHOCK

You are now having to share your life with two strangers, the bank manager AND the baby, and perhaps for the first time in your life together (perhaps not) your loved one is much more interested in someone else than you, and I'm not talking about the bank manager. This might well lead to Post-Natal Depression and, if you are very unlucky, your wife might get it too.

After those first few euphoric days when mother and baby are still in hospital and once again everyone at work, if you go to work, is insisting on buying you drinks, you suddenly find yourself in a totally unexpected domestic situation, i.e. having to do all the housework and cooking and providing hospitality for the coachloads of family and friends who are arriving by the hour to admire your new houseguest and who, for the most part, ignore you completely. Your social life is in tatters. A good night's sleep is a thing of dim and distant memory. You can't keep awake at work. You are even more overdrawn. You have become a celibate.

Is this, you may well find yourself asking, really what all the last nine months has been about? And is this, you may well also ask, really what the next nine months is going to be about? The answer to both these questions is, broadly, yes and, in my experience, there is only one way to cope with it at the same time as keeping both happy and sane.

YOU SUDDENLY FIND YOURSELF IN A TOTALLY UNEXPECTED DOMESTIC SITUATION.

Plunge in, with both feet. Don't run away to the golf course or pub, but stay at home and devote your time to Good Works. Change the nappies. Wash the nappies. Burp the baby. Bath the baby. Plead to be allowed to do the washing-up. Become totally indispensable.

In this way you will at least be able to have some control over your new life. Not much. But a little.

The first and (I found) most painful penalty arising from the presence of our new houseguest was lack of sleep. Mo, who had to breastfeed Tom, was suffering even more than I but then at least she didn't have to answer to a news-editor at work who breathed fire if deadlines were missed or performances slightly below par. I was doing a good deal of television work at this time and viewers kept writing in about the bags under my eyes and asking if I had some terrible terminal disease. Some of the stories I was given to cover didn't exactly help. I had spent a very hard day working in the BBC's *Breakfast Time* office, for example, and was just about to leave for home, and several tons of dirty nappies, when aforesaid news-editor grabbed me by the collar and said: 'Ah! Farrell!'

Now I don't know about you but, in my experience, if a news-editor grabs you by the collar and says 'Ah!' then bad news is imminent, and so it proved to be. Not, of course, that he came straight out with it. Oh no.

'How's the new baby, Farrell?'

'Fine, sir, and thank you so much for being kind enough to take such an interest', I replied in the forlorn hope that grovelling might help avert impending bad news.

'Good, good. Ever been to the Scilly Isles?'

I said how kind it was of him to enquire, but no, I had never had the pleasure.

'Excellent. I'd like you to go'.

'Thank you, sir, I . . .'

'Now.'

'Now?'

'Now.'

I thought this slightly unreasonable of him, having been awake most of the night thanks to Tom's incessant nocturnal activity and having now completed a twelve-hour day. Tactfully I tried to hint at this point.

'It is 7.30 p.m., sir, and my wife . . .'

'And take as many rolls of lavatory paper as you can carry, Farrell. Great story. Good luck. Well done, laddie.'

I ought to explain at this point that, because of a strike by seamen, there had been no ferry to the Scilly Isles for several weeks and supplies of most essentials on the islands were getting very low. Petrol and even bread were being rationed and stocks of loo rolls were exhausted. I had to drive down to Penzance right away, fly by helicopter to the Scilly Isles on the next available flight with as many loo rolls as I could carry, meet a film crew there and shoot a short film in which I had to do a piece-to-camera dishing out the loo rolls to relieved islanders. I had often wondered what it was that took me into journalism in the first place and at about this moment the question once again floated to mind.

At first light the following morning, having bought about 120 loo rolls in seven vast carrier-bags from an astonished late-night London chemist and driven the three hundred and fifty miles to Penzance, I arrived at the heliport and checked in.

'Any baggage, sir?' said the British Airways girl politely, eyeing with some suspicion the seven carrier-bags. 'Would you mind getting it weighed?'

I joined a queue of other passengers waiting with their baggage and rather self-consciously (on account of the seven bags, you understand) shuffled forward until I reached the front.

‘Right, sir, put your bags on the weighing machine, please’, said the baggage man, also with a suspicious glint in his eye, and when I did so, he looked puzzled. ‘That’s very odd’, he muttered. ‘Would you mind taking your bags off again?’

I removed the bags and the man looked more puzzled still. ‘I’m so sorry, they don’t seem to be registering on the balance. Bloody machine must be broken.’

The soles of my feet started tingling with embarrassment. Should I tell him what the bags contained? Behind me, in the queue, people were getting irritated. There were murmurings of ‘What’s the delay?’, ‘What’s going on?’ etc.

Eventually the man went off and returned with a colleague, and together they squatted down and squinted at the dial on the machine.

‘Put your bags on now please.’

I piled the bags on once again, and once again nothing registered. The two men now decided that they must call a maintenance engineer.

It was at this point that I felt compelled to own up.

‘Look, I’m terribly sorry but perhaps the reason they’re not registering is because they are all full of rolls of lavatory paper.’

‘All seven, sir?’

‘All seven.’

Unfortunately the shortage of loo paper on the islands had not been publicised and the two men started to back away from me as they might an escaped prisoner from Broadmoor.

Behind me the peasants were beginning to revolt, now shouting things like: ‘Get on with it you silly old bugger, we’re going to miss the flight’, and ‘Get that lunatic out of the way!’ in that charming way people in Britain have when they are standing in queues. This was a moment, I decided at once, for decisive action.

'Actually, I'm from the BBC.'

For anyone who's never worked for the BBC before I ought to explain that the letters BBC have a most dramatic effect on most people. Over the years I have found that the mere mention of the BBC is a licence for the most bizarre and apparently insane behaviour. You can walk around the streets dressed as a gigantic spaceman or ask passers-by whether they make love more often in hot weather – both of which I'm afraid I have done – and if they think you are from the BBC they won't bat an eyelid.

It did the trick, as usual. The two men nodded in unison, in sudden comprehension.

'Oh the BBC? Why didn't you say so before? Through you go, squire – next please!'

I flew to the islands, spent all day being filmed handing out lavatory paper to astonished islanders, got the last flight back to the mainland, drove back to London, edited the film throughout the night, made sure it was transmitted on the programme next morning, and then went home for what was laughingly described as 'sleep'. This period of so-called 'sleep' coincided with Tom suffering an acute attack of wind. He was totally inconsolable, the poor child screamed all day, despite our very earnest endeavours and that night, on one of the very few occasions since Tom's arrival when we had invited around friends for the evening, father and son both fell fast asleep at almost exactly the same moment: son whilst tucked up in his little cot upstairs, father right in the middle of dinner, an achievement on my part which went down extremely badly with aforesaid spouse but which amused our guests to such an extent that I have never been allowed to forget it.

If you really do have to work hard during the day, what,

I FELL FAST ASLEEP IN THE MIDDLE OF DINNER WHICH AMUSED OUR GUESTS TO SUCH AN EXTENT THAT I HAVE NEVER BEEN ALLOWED TO FORGET IT.

I wondered, is the minimum amount of sleep required each night before your performance and efficiency is noticeably affected? To find out I went to the sleep laboratories in Loughborough University, where a team of scientists spend their time doing a series of sadistic experiments, like keeping volunteers awake for days at a time to see how sleep deprivation affects them, and it appears that, whilst a severe lack of sleep dramatically reduces your ability to cope with monotonous, boring tasks like motorway driving, it has virtually no effect whatsoever during critical or even vital moments of activity, like putting out a kitchen fire or shooting a rifle, which you can do just as well as if you have been sleeping like Rip Van Winkle for a couple of months. This of course is good news if you are a fireman or an assassin and have a terrible night with the baby but if you are an accountant or lorry-driver forget it.

The results of these experiments have now been used to explain the mysterious disappearance of a number of aircraft during the last war. Bomber crews, often suffering a chronic lack of sleep following night after night of continuous operations, would be able to fly to their targets without any difficulty and drop their bombs perfectly but, on the long journey home, without adrenalin and nervous anticipation to keep them alert, they would often go to sleep, sometimes simultaneously, so that the entire crew would fall asleep at precisely the same moment and the aircraft would crash.

Often, it seems, people believe that they are sleeping far less than they really are. One woman went along to Loughborough convinced that she never slept at all and, as evidence of this, she stated quite categorically that she could always hear the town clock chime out every hour throughout the night. When tested by the boffins it emerged that actually she slept MOST of the night, with her body clock waking her up automatically seconds before the clock chimed out and then sending her straight back to sleep as soon as it had finished. The body clock's control over sleep is amazingly powerful, which is why a mother will often wake up in the middle of the night seconds before her child begins to cry out for its regular feed and, if you are anything like me, you will end up doing the same thing.

Once the baby is weaned, or if it is on a bottle, it might be an idea to split the night into separate shifts, during which you each take responsibility for the hollerin' brat in turn. A system that has been suggested, and which seems to work quite well, is this: on alternate nights, one of you gets up for the baby between 12 midnight and 6 o'clock and the other before midnight and between 6 and 8 o'clock in the morning. In this way you will both be guaranteed six hours undisturbed sleep every other night and, if this doesn't sound like much to you, then consider yourself lucky – to the parents of a really sleepless child, six hours every other night is the equivalent to paradise on earth.

The only real consolation, which may or may not be of help to those with a new-born baby, is that most sleeping problems have ended by the age of four and all should have finished by the age of five.

Only a few more years to go!

* * *

Let us now turn our attention to a subject which may not have played much of a part in your life recently. There is an old medical school joke which goes something like this:

Keen young medical student anxious to impress consultant: How long after delivery, sir, may the father consider suggesting intercourse?

Consultant: Most well-brought up fathers wait at least until after the after-birth has arrived.

Quite apart from the fact that, physically, your wife has been mangled and ravaged by the arrival of the baby, it is quite possible that the dramatic oscillations in her hormonal balance have quite put her off the idea of sex completely for weeks/months/years/ever. Even after the rigours of the episiotomy have faded into history and she is back in tip-top physical condition, the thought of once again indulging in the very activity which started the whole ghastly business off in the first place might send her into mild delirium tremens and, in a way, you can't blame her.

You, on the other hand, may not only be feeling slightly neglected and well down her list of priorities in the pecking order, but have just been through a period of intense celibacy during which any seed-spilling on your part has probably been non-existent, and now endless cold showers and five-mile jogs are no longer doing the trick. What's to be done?

The answer is that you may well have to set about seducing her in just the same way, if that was the way it was, you made love to her the very first time. Like a shy maiden lacking in confidence she must be won over anew. Woo her. Buy flowers. Learn the violin and play it 'neath her window. Take her for evening walks in shady bowers. Be gentle.

The *Kama Sutra*, written in the third century AD, has some interesting suggestions on this subject which you may like to try. In an effort to arouse the woman, it says, a man should pursue casual physical contact, like holding hands and touching feet, and should 'press a finger of her hand between his toes when she happens to be washing his feet'.

Very sound advice.

The pleasure-room, we are told, should be decorated with flowers and be fragrant with perfumes, and the couple should sing together and talk suggestively of things which would be considered as coarse, and not be mentioned generally in society. At last, when the woman is overcome with love and desire, sexual union may proceed – this last idea being a subject on which, as you may expect, the *Kama Sutra* has some more useful tips:

> Blows with the fist should be given on the back of the woman while she is sitting in the lap of the man, and she should give the man blows in return, abusing the man as if she were angry, and making the cooing and weeping sounds. While the woman is engaged in congress the space between the breasts should be struck with the back of the hand, slowly at first, and then proportionately to the increasing excitement, until the end.

So far so good? For the next bit you may need to practise a little on your own beforehand; avoid doing so in public places.

> At this time the sounds 'Hin' and others may be made ... when the man, making the sound 'Phat', strikes the woman on the head, with the fingers of his hand a little contracted, it is called Prasritaka, which means striking with the fingers of the hand a little contracted. In this case the appropriate sounds are the cooing sounds, the sound 'Phat' and the sound 'Phut' in the interior of the mouth.

Do let me know how you get on.

* * *

A word here about another pair of formidable characters who you may feel are beginning to take over your life, to bully, worry and threaten you, and here I am referring not to either bank manager or baby; I mean the district nurse and health visitor. It is quite imperative that you know exactly when they are coming because, if you don't, you can be sure that they will arrive just as you are emerging from the bedroom with an appalling hangover or when you are in the middle of a terrible, violent argument.

Actually, the first time you both come up against this kind of character is immediately after the birth of your baby when the sister responsible for such matters will cruise over to your wife whilst she is still in bed recovering from the ravages of the labour-ward and start grilling her about birth-control. This struck me as bizarre. Why a woman who has just gone through the best part of a year in the agonies and ecstasies of having a child would, the very next morning after its delivery, really want to start discussing contraception and all that pulverised-mule-testicle and vinegar-on-the-penis stuff beats me, but then I suppose the authorities for once have you trapped and know that you are unlikely to leap out of bed and run for home – especially if you have had an episiotomy– and that you are a captive audience for the subject of unwanted children. Or maybe they just believe that, with the experience so fresh in your mind, it is the ideal moment to point out how unnecessary the whole business is if you are not serious about it. Anyway I can tell you that, after just having her lower deck torn apart by baby, doctors and midwives armed with steel scissors, poor Mo was not in an ideal mood to start arguing about the relative merits of the cap over the coil, and I don't blame her.

Anyway, once you are all safely home and free of aggressive females brandishing packets of French letters and the like, the district nurse may come to see you every day to check on the health of mother and baby, and the health visitor once or twice a week to make sure the baby's not driving you around the twist and you are coping with your new life. Some parents regard the health visitor particularly as an unwanted spy, and I suppose intelligence-gathering on your circumstances is part of her brief and, in some cases, a very necessary one too. The best way of handling the health visitor is to use her to your advantage. Pick her brains for advice. Use her experience. We used to store up a list of questions for when she arrived and bombard the poor woman with them until she couldn't get out of the front door fast enough. Do make sure you brief siblings about 'getting on the right side' of the nurse or health visitor. Recently the three-year-old daughter of a friend announced to the district nurse who had come to inspect the new baby that she was 'helping Daddy mend the fucking lawnmower'.

After a few weeks of living with all these strangers, to wit: new baby; a woman who thanks to motherhood is now quite unlike the one you decided to live with all that time ago; bank manager; district nurse; health visitor; a mother-in-law who is now on the verge of taking up residence with you; and old Auntie Laura whom you thought died years ago and who suddenly can't keep away, something weird begins to happen to you. Imperceptibly at first of course; nature's too subtle to keep too high a profile. But happening all the same.

At first, I couldn't put my finger on it. Then I realised, quite unexpectedly, quite dramatically, one evening when I was just finishing a hard day's paperwork and 'phone-bashing at the office. It was the kind of thing which had never happened to me before, and when it did, I can tell you it shook me.

I had packed up the things on my desk and had stuffed a huge pile of papers into my briefcase. I stood up, slowly and wearily. I was thirsty. I remember looking at my watch. 6.17 p.m. precisely.

A group of colleagues walked past my desk and one of them slapped me on the back, quite hard I remember. I turned round and he said: 'Your turn to buy the first round, Nigel.' Just like that. Nothing sinister, or suspicious. Just those few, apparently innocuous words, delivered with almost a light-hearted ring to them.

I turned and, without smiling, I spoke. I remember now the stream of evening sunlight splashed across the desks in the room. I remember the rows of empty seats that once, much, much earlier in the day had been teeming with busy people, leading busy, busy lives.

When the words came they sounded as though they were being spoken by someone else, someone I'd never met before. Even now, the recollection of it all sends a shudder down my spine.

'No, thanks', I heard myself say. 'I think I'll go straight home if it's all the same to you.'

I'll never forget the looks on their faces.

After that moment of sudden self-awareness, life was never quite the same. Work, far from being the blessed relief from the noisy intrusion of so many strangers, became a bit of a chore. Home life, with all the superficial appearance of a true living hell, took on a strange appeal I had never known before.

Shortly afterwards, my boss told me to fly to Paris and make a film about what it was like to stay in the world's most expensive hotel. Arduous job, mine, as you have probably noticed.

Just in case you didn't know, the world's most expensive hotel is just off the Champs Elysees in Paris. It is called the Nova-Park Elysees and, a couple of years ago, when we went, the prices ranged from about £600 to £3,500 per night. The biggest suites had annexes for your bodyguards but I was given one of the real cheapos, a mere two-storey

WORK BECAME A CHORE, HOME LIFE, WITH ALL THE SUPERFICIAL APPEARANCE OF A TRUE LIVING HELL, TOOK ON A STRANGE APPEAL.

suite stuffed with antique furniture, quadrophonic speakers in every corner, telexes etc. We flew to Charles de Gaulle airport and were picked up in the hotel's Rolls-Royce – bullet-proof, naturally – and the first thing I did when I arrived was to go to my suite for a jacuzzi. They don't have baths at the Nova-Park, just vast jacuzzis the size of a small swimming-pool in each room, with rows of hot-air jets which attack those parts of you lying beneath the surface of the water.

Whilst I was waiting for the jacuzzi to fill up, I lay on the bed, which was about as big as a tennis court and was divided into different sections, each of which would go up or down at the press of a button on a small control panel on the bedside table so if, for example, you wanted to raise your left leg a few inches you merely pressed the button and the rest was done for you. I turned on the hi-fi radio with which you could pick up every station in Europe and, sipping a glass of champagne from one of the half-dozen or so bottles liberally dotted about the place, I slipped into the jacuzzi.

Strangely the radio was tuned to the BBC, Radio 4 in fact, and as I lay sitting in the jacuzzi, with hot-air bubbles doing extraordinary things to my undercarriage, and sipping champagne in the world's most expensive hotel, the Archers' signature tune suddenly started to belt out from the quadrophonic speakers and there was Clarrie giving Joe and Eddie Grundy a bollocking for getting drunk at The Bull. Not for the first time I found myself thinking that this was a pretty bizarre way of earning a living.

Still, for the next few luxurious days at least, Paris and all its delights lay stretched out before me. Time to finish the jacuzzi, pop down for a sauna, wander across the road to sample the night-life of the Champs Elysees or perhaps summon up the bullet-proof Rolls for a spin down the floodlit Boulevard de Saint-Germain.

There was just one thing which really did spoil the trip. I spent the entire time genuinely wishing I was at home with Mo and Tom. Even though he was still only an 'orrible little bundle of screams and wet nappies I was already missing the little bugger.

5

PRACTICALITIES

There are quite a number of gadgets about which may help make life at home a little nearer to the kind of blissful civilisation you used to enjoy – remember? – and some of them are worth looking at it in detail, particularly the first on my shopping list. This is something you can usually hire by the week or month, is often made in Sweden, although the French and Germans do a pretty competitive model, and can be extremely attractive to look at. I'm talking about an au pair which these days is not very expensive in terms of pay but often very expensive in terms of space, time, food and arguments with your wife.

The Victorians actually went one better than au pairs and, because bottle-feeding was regarded as the ultimate in degeneration, would hire a wet-nurse. The wet-nurse should be in her twenties, perfectly healthy and with 'full-round breasts' and nipples 'erectile and firm' and you may wish to use the same criteria when choosing an au pair. According to the *Household Physician of 1885*, any girl applying to be a wet-nurse should be

> ... carefully examined to ensure that she is free from any communicable disease such as consumption or syphilis. For this purpose her teeth, gums, throat, skin and hair should be inspected. Her breasts should be firm, not flat or flabby, and the nipples should be

free from fissures. Her milk should be examined, and should be sweetish and blue-ish white. On standing it should yield a considerable quantity of cream.

Most of us have to make do with babysitters, of course, and here it is important to remember that all babysitters, whatever their age, experience or sex, are inveterate liars. No babysitter has ever yet been known to tell the truth, or at least the complete truth. They will spend the whole evening pulling their hair out with worry about your child, go through agonies on whether or not to call the doctor, experience long-term damage to their hearing because of the screaming, be unable to find any of your food, alcohol and coffee and, even if they do, won't understand how to turn the kettle on, let the fire go out, spend the whole evening freezing with cold and quivering with fear because they are convinced they can hear a burglar climbing in through the bathroom window, miss the final episode of *Dallas* so that they will never know what really happened and being told just isn't the same, consider infanticide, suffer momentary bouts of schizophrenia and acute loss of self-confidence and memory and, when you walk in at midnight, just as the baby finally goes off to sleep for the first time, the babysitter will force a perfectly hideous smile in your direction and before you have had a chance to ask, will say 'I've had a marvellous evening, the baby's been as good as gold, no really he has, I needn't have been here at all, ha! hope you've had a super time, no he really couldn't have been better, thank you so much for asking me, don't hesitate to ask me again, I'd be only too delighted', and be out of your front door so fast all you'll see is the dust settling.

I once knew a couple who were actually quite good friends of ours who were quite prepared to leave their baby alone in their flat while they went out for an hour or two to the pub, which they did frequently. 'No problem', they said. 'If there's a fire or something the next-door neighbour would rescue him.' I protested at this extraordinary attitude but they took no notice. Rather optimistically I suppose I assumed this was a very unusual case but amazingly, three days later, I worked with a cameraman who had just completed shooting an interview with An Extremely Well-Known Celebrity at his home who had suggested exactly the same thing. Oddly enough, he popped up on television recently, introducing an item about baby-care.

My brother-in-law, who is clever with nuts and bolts and wires and old bits of metal, designed and made a most effective baby-rocker. It consists of a small electrical engine screwed on to the back bar of the pram from which extends a revolving metal arm. On the end of this is a bloody great lump of metal. You switch it on, the arm begins to go round and the circular movement of the bloody great lump of metal is enough to gently rock pram and baby. There are different speeds to the device and on 'maximum' the movement was quite dramatic, so that I constantly expected a pale little seasick face to appear from somewhere within the blankets and vomit over the side. In fact the thing worked like a dream, putting Tom out for several hours at a time. It once nearly put me out, too. I dropped a safety-pin by the end of the pram and, as I bent down to pick it up, the rotating bloody great lump of metal, which unfortunately was switched to 'maximum', clocked me on the side of the head. It felt as though I'd been clouted with one of those gigantic steel balls from a demolition crane and I think I still have a lump there.

A few months ago I met a woman whose baby would only ever sleep with the vacuum-cleaner on. Her hearing has never been the same since but she's got the cleanest house I have ever stepped into.

Baby-bouncers – in which baby is suspended in mid-air by a huge piece of elastic hanging from an open doorway – can be very useful, although don't forget where your baby is when you are fed up with the draught and slam the door shut. On my suggestion, my brother-in-law is now working on a version for adults.

Remember that many so-called 'child-proof' gadgets can be adult-proof too. Having spent the evening proudly screwing on one of those adjustable wooden gates designed to prevent Tom falling down our very steep set of stairs, I woke up in the middle of the night desperate for a glass of water and, totally naked and still half asleep, walked straight onto the dark landing and straight into the gate, tipping over it like some Olympic pole-vaulter and crashing half-way down the stairs.

Of course, the ultimate baby-gadget is nothing more complicated than a piece of usually-tatty yellow fur, very roughly shaped into arms (with no hands), legs (with no feet) and head (with no mouth). Quite what the appeal of the Teddy Bear is, and has been over the years, I have never quite understood but its effect on calming harassed young children, and consequently their harassed parents, is still as dramatic as ever. Do not underestimate the importance of your child's Teddy. If you value your sanity, guard the wretched thing as your own life.

My niece, Whizzie, had a worn and faded little Teddy with a rather revolting withered arm that she worshipped and adored with a passionate intensity. The arm, I must explain, became withered because Whizzie held it with an iron-like grip for every moment of her waking hours, usually sucking the very end of it as well, so that in time the arm had all its fur rubbed and sucked off; the only time Whizzie and Ted With The Withered Arm were ever, ever separated was when Whizzie was in a deep sleep and one was able to

NEVER UNDERESTIMATE THE IMPORTANCE OF YOUR CHILDS' TEDDY BEAR.

prize open her fingers and extract the rather unsavoury specimen for bunging in the washing-machine.

Well, yes, you've guessed it, one terrible, terrible day Ted With The Withered Arm went missing. Whizzie had fallen asleep while being pushed through the park in her pushchair and it was only when she got home and woke up for tea that the disaster became apparent. Within a few minutes there was Panic and Chaos à la Dante's Inferno as Mum and Dad frantically searched the house, and then later the car, and then the park, and then the entire town. But alas! Ted With The Withered Arm had either been kidnapped or decided to go his own sweet way and poor Whizzie was inconsolable.

That evening Whizzie's Mum and Dad held a crisis meeting. Trying to keep cool heads they rationally itemised the options. Finally, with the child sobbing upstairs, Dad hit upon an Ingenious Plan.

'Simple', said Dad. 'We'll buy a new Teddy.'

'But it won't have a Withered Arm!' pointed out Mum.

'Then we shall Wither one of them!'

Have you ever tried to wither a Teddy's arm? Not easy, I'm told. In this case they would have had to rub and suck the new Ted's arm continuously for about six months to make it look authentic. Dad would have had to give up work.

Then, after several hours of negotiations, Dad hit on Ingenious Plan Mark 2 and, rushing upstairs to Whizzie's bedroom, he put it to her.

What had happened, he explained, trying to contain his excitement, was that Ted With The Withered Arm's withered arm had become so withered he had had to go to hospital for repairs. He would probably be in hospital for a week or so and would emerge from the Teddy Ward after a lengthy and complicated operation carried out by the world's leading furry-withered-arm specialist with two perfect arms again, just like new.

Whizzie accepted this version of events after some persuasion and next morning Dad contacted Mother-In-Law who had originally supplied Ted With The Withered Arm, although of course when she had bought him from the toy shop he had been Ted With Two Perfectly Normal Arms, and Mother-In-Law returned to the shop to buy another, same colour, two normal arms please. But when she got to the shop, catastrophe! They had sold out only a few days before.

'Where are the Teddies made?' enquired Mother-In-Law.

'Guernsey', came the depressing reply.

Now such was the devotion of child and Ted that no one in the family was prepared to shed their responsibility. It so happened that Mother-In-Law had a brother living in Guernsey, Uncle Jim, who was telephoned without delay and instructed to make haste to the Teddy Bear factory and purchase one, sending it back by the very next post. Every morning for the next week Dad got up early to intercept the post and, after a time, his vigilance paid off. One day the postman arrived bearing a brown-paper package; Dad ripped it open and inside was Ted With No Withered Arms At All. Quickly he took the Ted out, bandaged its arm, put it back in the package, placed it carefully on the doorstep and ran around to the back of the house and in through the back door.

'I wonder if the post has arrived yet Whizzie? Shall I go to the porch and see?' he asked when Whizzie, still very mournful after her tragic loss, was brought down for breakfast.

'Good heavens, look what the postman has brought, Whizzie! It must be Ted With The Withered Arm back from his operation!'

Carefully Whizzie opened the box and unwrapped the new Teddy, and, casting a very suspicious glance indeed at the bandage, began a careful examination before finally bursting into tears.

'What on earth's the matter?' asked Mum and Dad in dismay.

'Not my Ted!' protested Whizzie, hurling Ted With The Unwithered Arm firmly to the ground.

'But Whizzie, how on earth do you know it's not your Ted?'

'Wrong colour!' announced the tearful child.

May that be a lesson to you.

* * *

Undoubtedly the most handy piece of equipment to have around with a new baby is your wife's bosom, if you will pardon the expression, because the fruits of it are not only superbly nutritious but do more to save your labour than all the rest of the gadgets at your disposal put together. Nicer to look at than the others, too.

It was only when I saw other new parents less fortunate than us carrying around cartloads full of bottles, rubber teats, sterilising gear and gawd knows what that I realised how wonderful it is to be married to a woman with an apparently inexhaustible supply of milk. Mo kept Tom and Alex going for ten months and could no doubt have done the same for a few cohorts of other children. We never even possessed a bottle, let alone used one. Wherever you are, at whatever time, all that is required is the whipping-out of a breast and think no more about it. No boiling water needed. No washing up necessary. Nothing to forget or leave at home.

Happy, gurgling child. Happy gurgling father. Not every woman has a massive reservoir of the stuff, of course, and it is not ideal for those mothers anxious to get back to work, but if she can make supply meet demand encourage her to do so. There are lots of little spin-offs in this deal for you, too. Not only can you still continue to enjoy a great social life through being so mobile and unencumbered, whilst she's still breastfeeding but there is nothing you can do to help feed baby if he wakes at night (shame!) and, whilst bond 'twixt mother and child forged by breast means that she can never have much time away from the baby, there's really no excuse for you to turn down that invitation for a day at Lord's or Epsom (poor you!). Mo is one of twins and her mum used to breastfeed both simultaneously, although quite what happened if the telephone rang or someone came to the door whilst this extraordinary feat was in progress I have never dared ask.

Breastfeeding in public places can sometimes be difficult but Mo used to be discreet about it and frankly most people don't even notice. I have seen some women positively waving their breasts about in the air when breastfeeding, like overweight go-go dancers, which, in somewhere like a restaurant, can result in long-term damage, like putting you off vol-au-vent for life, but nobody ever objected to us and there's no reason why they should. The only problem we encountered was the fact that some men find the sight of a mother feeding her baby excruciatingly embarrassing. We had a friend call on us one day and when he saw Tom at Mo's breast he first froze and then turned so red I could almost feel the heat of his face from the other side of the room. For the next half an hour, whilst he finished his drink and we talked about this and that, he not only didn't dare look at Mo again but he didn't look at anything within a ten-foot radius of her. It was as though she was radio-active;

all very odd really because whilst looking in totally the opposite direction he continued talking to her. She would ask him about work or his family and, with his eyes fixed firmly onto the lightstand, curtainrail, carpet or line of trees through the window on the horizon, he would struggle to reply.

It must have been agony, and I know something of what he felt myself because a year or two ago I visited a nudist camp, not, I hasten to add, for fun, but to do some interviews. It is a very strange feeling talking to people who are totally naked. I remained fully clothed, of course, and found that, like our poor visitor, I was prepared to look at anything save the bodies in question. Walking past the swimming pool and tennis courts when I arrived I stared at the sky, the tops of trees, the grass and my shoes. When I was recording the interviews I fixed my gaze onto the eyes of the person I was talking to, never, ever daring to look down, not even to look at their teeth, despite the fact that I was only too aware in some cases of some interesting undulations on the lower periphery of vision. Rather like standing on the edge of a cliff and having to fight the urge to leap off. Afterwards some of my more lecherous and less well brought-up colleagues came out with some choice questions such as 'Cor! You lucky bastard, did you see any bodies you really, really fancied!' and I had to reply in all honesty that I had seen no bodies of any description at all.

For the first time since your own childhood – and for many, many years to come – you will now have to start a) buying toys and b) playing with them. No matter what you buy, your baby will expect you to play with his toys because this is vastly more entertaining than having to play with them himself, so choose things that you think will amuse you, not him. Tom used to love mobiles, those things which take you several years to work out how to put together and then hang from the ceiling gently moving in the air currents. Tom's favourite was an agricultural scene in which the sun was rising over a field of corn and a farmer was leaning on an old gate watching his sheep. It came in about one hundred and fifty different pieces and, when I had finally managed to assemble it, I found the only way to mount it was to climb onto a very high bookshelf which promptly collapsed just as I reached the summit. Tom found this extremely amusing and lay on his back giggling like a baby hyena and frantically kicking his little feet in the air, an action which, under the circumstances, I felt like doing myself, and which he repeated every time he subsequently looked at the mobile. Kept him quiet for hours. Fitting a new bookshelf kept me quiet for hours, too. Alex's favourite toy as a baby was a thing that looked like Paddington Bear which was attached to the inside of the cot. Damn clever device, too. When doting grannies and aunts bent down to kiss her, Alex would reach out to a small piece of string hanging down from the bear which, when pulled hard, kicked his arms and legs into the air. The ensuing cries of pain as bear's boot came into sharp contact with aunt's temple – a very sensitive area of the anatomy, actually, as those who remember that story in the Bible about the geezer whose wife drove a peg through his temple because she was upset about something or other will testify – never failed to produce whoops of joy from our daughter. Incidentally, your children will expect you to play with their toys for many years to come, so this rule doesn't just apply to babies. I have passed many a happy evening in recent years changing Barbie dolls and serving behind the counter at Postman Pat's Post Office shop.

This might be a good moment to draw your attention to a relatively new and very painful affliction peculiar to new fathers which was highlighted recently in the learned medical journal, *The Lancet*. Its called Purpura Cyclops

(Sucker-Daddy Syndrome) and this is what two eminent cardiovascular consultants had to say about it:

Epidemiology: both cases occurred in young fathers of first-born infant sons.
Causal agent: child's rattle or similar toy mounted on a rubber sucker.
Pathogenesis: while playing with his child, the father sticks the sucker, unicorn-fashion, on to the centre of his forehead; subsequently, he is unable to remove it without a violent wrench.
Disease progression: multiple petechiae progress to confluent bruising or purpura with the usual progression of colour changes over several days.
Diagnostic criteria: a perfectly circular bruise in the centre of the forehead.
Prognosis and complications: complete recovery, but temporary embarrassment.
Treatment: none; heavy make-up might be applied in any social emergency.
Prevention: the condition could be prevented by selling leaky suckers or piercing a hole to provide an air vent; alternatively, this could be done to the parent's forehead.

This article produced an amazing amount of correspondence, uncovering at least another eighteen recorded cases within a month, amongst them two fathers who reported getting the condition after mimicking Daleks from Dr Who.

I, too, have suffered a severe attack of Purpura Cyclops, a particularly hazardous condition for anyone who earns a living from appearing on television. Much to Tom's amusement I was only able to pull off my sucker by closing the living-room door over the end of it and pulling my whole body with all my strength, an operation I was in the midst of just when the babysitter arrived. The following day I had to go and interview the yachtswoman and authoress Claire Francis and I found myself talking to her with my hand constantly over my forehead, as though I was constantly in deep thought about some insoluble problem. Inevitably my attention slipped for a moment and Miss Francis, seeing this great pulsating red orb on my forehead burst into laughter and, much to my relief, explained that precisely the same thing had happened to her a month or two before. The cameraman was kind enough to shoot me entirely in profile.

You have been warned.

* * *

A word here about redecorating the kitchen. This needs to be done shortly BEFORE your baby begins to feed himself and not, as commonly assumed, after. You must do your research before deciding how and what to do with your walls and most important here is to make sure you know what exactly is your baby's favourite food. Alex, for example, eventually came to adore butterscotch whip. She wanted nothing else and, in the early stages of learning to feed herself, would fling bucketfuls of the stuff all over her head, body, high-chair, walls, ceilings and floor. So obviously we rapidly decided to recover the walls in a hessian cloth precisely the same colour. A friend whose child took a liking to strawberry mousse went in for a delightful bright red wallpaper.

Its also very important at this stage to TALK to your baby, even though the baby can't talk back and the conversation will remain pretty much one-sided. This is the only way they ever learn. Constant repetition of key words may drive you bonkers but it will mean your baby has a head-start in language. One recent American study showed that, on average, fathers talked to their young infants for thirty-seven seconds each day. So it doesn't take much to be above average. Also smile as much as possible. So keen was I for Tom to copy me and smile back that I spent most of the first year of his life with a constant smile on my face. It became unconsciously fixed, like a piece of sculpture, even when I was having a terrible time or in receipt of bad news. At work my boss thought I had achieved an Inner Peace which made me worthy of more responsibility and respect and all my friends thought I had gone around the twist.

Don't forget that babies are also passports to new friendships. The whole world is interested in babies. After all those roguish bachelor years, you have finally become integrated, accepted into the community. Old men who have always regarded you as an ageing hooligan start patting you on the head. Old ladies swoon at even the ugliest baby and look at their fathers with a new respect. You have finally achieved what society expected of you. You can hold your head up high. Soon you will be invited to help out at the Church Fete and stand for the Parish Council.

Take the pram or pushchair into the park and you will also inevitably and unavoidably meet a huge range of young mothers, all of them interested in comparing notes, and many no doubt feeling lonely or neglected by their own husbands. Proceed here with caution.

6

SELF-PROPELLED BABY

Just as you are beginning to get used to your new life for the first time since the trauma of the birth, just as you have mastered a sleep pattern which begins to reduce the size of those coalsacks beneath your eyes, just as you are at last starting to get back on top of work; just, in short, as everything is beginning to look just a little rosier, the world a brighter place and life with your new houseguest pretty tickety-boo after all, your baby starts to develop a horrendous characteristic which immediately makes most of the knowledge you have gained about him through cruel experience out of date in a moment.

He becomes mobile.

At first you won't even notice it. You will get home one evening, walk into the kitchen, kiss the baby lying on the floor at one end of the room, chat to your wife, pour a large whisky and then, quite suddenly, you will notice that your baby isn't sitting at that end of the room at all but, by some miraculous means, has leapt right across to the other end of the room. This you know is impossible. Your baby can't even sit up on his own, let alone crawl.

You look at the whisky. You shrug your shoulders. It has been a long day. You have another swig, and continue to chat away ten to the dozen. Then you notice something very strange indeed. Your baby has now apparently leapt back to the other end of the room to exactly where he was lying when you walked in. Now you worry. It's all beginning to resemble one of the later scenes in that ghastly film *The Exorcist*. Have you been overworking lately?

You don't want to alarm your wife, either about the possible supernatural abilities of your offspring or about the balance of your own mind so this time you keep chatting but fix your eyes onto the child and await developments. Nothing happens. You pick up the paper and pretend to read it. Then, just as your baby is convinced no one is watching him, he furtively begins to pull himself along the floor on his elbows, with his legs straight out behind him, and occasionally turning onto his back and rolling over and over. You are amazed and impressed. In no time at all he has crossed the entire room. Just like the SAS.

True mobility falls into two clearly-defined categories and you must take appropriate action in anticipation of both:

a) Crawling. Remove everything of value within a distance of three foot from the floor. Take out new 'All Risks' Household Insurance. Transfer stamp collection to vaults of local bank and nail up cat-flap.
b) Walking. Remove everything of value within a distance of five foot from the floor. Double value of existing 'All Risks' Household Insurance. Nail up window in baby's room. Let cat in.

Overnight your gurgling, happy little bundle securely tucked up in a cot has become a rampant wild animal hungry for stimuli. The repercussions of this can be appalling. We have one of those alarm radios which you can set so that it turns itself on in the morning and which we used to keep on the floor just by my side of the bed. I use the words 'used to' because it is not kept on the floor anymore. Oh, no. Not on the floor. It has these knobs on it, you see; one knob to adjust the station, one knob to change the time the alarm's set for, and one knob which controls volume. Big knobs, all of them; big, black shiny knobs.

I don't know whether you have ever been woken in the early hours of the morning by a really deafening sound. A shattering experience. The first reaction is that the world has just ended, roof's caved in, floor's collapsed, massive earthquakes. I don't like being woken like that, not at all.

On this occasion I was in the middle of a wonderful dream about gliding – it is a funny thing but I dream a great deal about being in the air and floating about the clouds aboard a beautiful flying machine or even just on my own, like some heavenly archangel – when I was nearly blasted from my bed by a booming voice screaming out at me from the loudspeaker of the radio, bellowing the words: 'BBC WORLD SERVICE NEWS AT 0300 HOURS GREENWICH MEAN TIME. FIRST THE ATTEMPTED COUP IN LIBERIA . . . .' Absolutely terrifying.

We don't keep the radio on the floor. Not any more.

Tom's first method of self-propulsion was a curious system, presumably inherited from some distant old relative, which involved sliding along the floor upright on his bottom, a sort of bum-shuffle in which he seemed able to pull himself forward by his feet and legs rather like a crab. It was very odd indeed to watch and meant that the seat of his dungarees and rompers were always shining, like busmen's trousers. We spent a small fortune on clothes, but didn't need to buy him new shoes for years and, thinking about it in retrospect, I suppose it was actually a pretty good way of getting about; after all, the stability he'd had which was brought about by the width of his bottom hugely exaggerated by bulging nappies meant that he constantly had both hands free as he moved, very handy for stuffing food in the mouth, or even hurling food at Daddy, and he had

BBC WORLD SERVICE NEWS AT 0300 HOURS GREENWICH MEAN TIME. FIRST, THE ATTEMPTED COUP IN LIBERIA...

far less distance to fall if he did lose his balance. It also must have done wonders for the development of his leg muscles. I tried it once and such was the pain I couldn't walk properly for a week, which was particularly embarrassing since the boss insisted on asking for a detailed explanation.

One other vital problem with this stage, which you simply cannot afford to underestimate, is that landlords are much less likely to let you into their pub if they think your child is mobile. I have never quite understood why it is fine to bring a three-month old baby into the bar but immoral to bring in a nine-month old, but then probably most landlords are more concerned about the complaints of their regulars than matters of morality. Finding ourselves suddenly barred from some of our favourite haunts we went through a period of trying to train Tom to regress whenever we went into a pub, i.e. stick him back into a pram and threaten him with dire consequences if he attempted to walk or talk but this approach rarely worked and is not recommended. In one pub Tom became so fractious that I thought we would be thrown out at any moment; in an effort to distract him while we finished our pints I jangled the car keys in front of him and when he reached to grab them I let him have them.

Mo and I then became involved in a heated discussion over something of Tremendous Significance To The Future Of The Universe like why I hadn't been doing my share of changing the nappies and it must have been ten minutes later when I asked Tom for the keys back. At this point he looked blank, an unusual expression for him; then he pointed to the main bar and said: 'Man!'

'You gave my keys to a man?' I asked in horror.

Tom grinned and pointed again at the bar.

'Man!'

It was a Sunday lunchtime in a very popular pub and in front of me, at a very rough estimate, there must have been somewhere between two and three hundred men.

We were late home that afternoon.

* * *

Tom was actually very unusual in being able to speak fluently long before he could walk properly, the complete opposite to most children, which I suppose says something about his priorities in life. In fact, by five or six months, most babies are able to carry out conversations which are quite remarkable in that they conform to every qualification of involved adult conversation except for the fact that the baby is talking total drivel.

What I mean is this: baby makes a sound, let's say something quite interesting like 'Booboo'; he then pauses in a very civilised kind of a way, to allow you to respond, which you politely do, along the lines perhaps of 'Is Booboo with us today?' Baby then considers this response and, after some thought, replies in turn: 'Aja!', adding, as an afterthought, 'Ippi Amam!' This will continue for as long as you are looking and talking to him; indeed I passed many happy hours talking to Tom and Alex in this way, never ceasing to be amazed that a complete lack of vocabulary did absolutely nothing to restrain their burning desire for a long chat. The speech patterns made it just like listening to a pair of foreigners in animated discussion; quite absorbing.

The next stage, equally entertaining, came when we suddenly noticed that the same bizarre word was being used over and over again when referring to something specific, i.e. Tom would look at a ball and say 'Yadje!' and continue saying 'Yadje!' every time he wanted the ball. Come to think of it, it is a good word, 'Yadje'. Much better than

BABIES ARE ABLE TO CARRY OUT CONVERSATIONS.

'ball'. After a time we found this a fascinating game to play, rather like going on a long holiday abroad without a phrasebook. We eventually worked out that 'Ni-noos' were the tops of fir trees; that 'Bellingtons' were one-legged monsters that lived beneath mountains; and, best of all, that the delicious word 'Zandon' – which mysteriously appeared whenever we passed a certain sort of traffic sign or someone holding an umbrella over their heads – actually meant a triangle*.

Many of their words were so much more interesting and fun than the real ones that Mo and I started using them in our everyday speech, which was confusing for outsiders, particularly those who didn't know us very well, like the milkman and tax inspector. I received some very strange looks when I kept asking the children if they'd like some farties to eat, after Alex's version of Smarties; after a time we noticed that the position was reversed, with the children using some of our words that they in turn didn't understand. These included the words 'The Somme' which we had used to describe the garden, in which at the time the builders were digging the trenches for foundations for a small extension and were having considerable difficulty because a series of typical British summer monsoons had reduced everything in sight to a sea of mud. The poor builders were constantly astonished by our two toddlers leaping about the trenches shouting 'The Somme! The Somme!' and one day, when seeking refuge inside for a cup of tea, said: 'Couple of very bright kiddies you have there, Mrs F.'

'Yes', replied Mrs F. quickly, keen not to shatter the illusion. 'They've both always been very interested in

* Yes, it took us a long time to work it out, too. Many road signs are of course triangular in shape; and next time you pass someone holding an umbrella look carefully and you'll notice that the ribbing divides the umbrella's material into triangular sections.

twentieth century history.'

The other major new development which, whether you like it or not, you will have to get involved in, is the exciting subject of potty-training. If you have been doing your share of the nappy-changing, as I'm sure you will have, then whilst in the short-term potty-training will definitely appear one of the more distasteful ordeals so far thought up by The Lord, in the long-term you will come to see its rewards as a prize well worth striving for, the lavatorial equivalent to a paradise on earth.

Try to sympathise with your baby. Try to remember what it is like to have bowels and bladder with minds of their own, and to help you achieve this make a Vindaloo with fourteen times the recommended amount of chillis. You must treat baby with the diplomacy and tact required for International Arms Negotiations. Praise him if he does well but don't, whatever you do, criticise him if it all goes horribly wrong because all the books say this can have dreadful consequences in later life, although whether they mean yours or his isn't clear. Don't expect too much too soon. Or, put another way, do expect too much too soon. Either way, don't make it sound too important, and be creative.

One evening, in desperation (but not of course showing it) I took Tom upstairs, threw all his teddies, bunnies, pandas, jumbos and other assorted representatives from the stuffed and furry animal kingdom into his Wendy House, along with a dozen plastic cups and bowls from the Teddy Picnic Set and two large potties. Tom and I then crawled in and, after placing him firmly on one of the potties and me on the other, I carefully arranged each of the teddies, bunnies, pandas and jumbos on a plastic cup or bowl so that each of us inside that Wendy House, without exception, was perched on some kind of receptacle. 'Right laddies', said I, with an air of what turned out to be misguided optimism. 'We all want to do something in the pot, don't we, even panda who hasn't been for days. He's actually bursting to do Daddy something in the pot and get a special prize, so let's all of us wait here on our lovely little pots for just as long as it takes to produce some kind of result. OK?'

Tom busied himself with a pile of plastic alphabet letters and I waited patiently, determined to stick it out until Tom had filled up his potty with something that would delight and satisfy me, and show Mo that it is perfectly possible to get a child to do what is required in a pot if only one applies oneself with common sense and imagination.

Well, what with the central heating on full and not much fresh air inside the little canvas Wendy House, after about twenty minutes I began to feel distinctly uncomfortable. I could feel the sides of the pot wearing great grooves in my buttocks but, determined to see it out to the bitter end, and to avoid the ignominy of going back downstairs to Mo with an empty pot, I started grunting and pushing in the hope that Tom would copy me. He found this immensely amusing. I then made grunting and pushing sounds on behalf of all the assembled animals, one by one, which certainly put the old vocal chords through their paces, and then continued with even more strenuous grunting and pushing of my own. There was still no sign of Tom producing anything whatsoever but suddenly I became aware of a fierce urgency gripping my bowels.

I only just made it to the loo.

7

THE AGONY OF SPEECH

Many years ago my parents took me and my brother into a restaurant. Now restaurants are not ideal places for very young children and, if you ever meet my mother, she will be only too delighted to tell you why.

On the other side of the restaurant to where the four of us were sitting there was a woman with extremely fat legs, a pair of really vast tree-trunks which fascinated my father, a doctor. Prompted by the amazing sight of this lady's lower half, he launched into a long explanation into the causes and effects of obesity. Whilst he was still in full flow my brother climbed down from his chair and waddled over to the poor woman in question. Just as it was too late, my poor parents realised what was happening but, although totally distraught, were unable to do anything to prevent their little bundle of joy from launching into the following: 'My Daddy, who is sitting over there, can you see him just behind that table? My Daddy, he says you have got the fattest pair of legs that he has ever, ever seen.' And then, after a short pause for effect, he added: 'And he should know, my Daddy. He's a doctor. Goodbye.'

From your point of view, speech brings potentially the most hazardous area of your child's formative years. You are now entering a period during which you are in constant danger of being embarrassed and humiliated in public.

"MY DADDY WHO IS SITTING OVER THERE SAYS YOU HAVE GOT THE FATTEST PAIR OF LEGS THAT HE HAS EVER SEEN...
MY DADDY SHOULD KNOW BECAUSE MY DADDY IS A DOCTOR."

Intimate secrets which you and your wife have shared for years without any fear of them ever being revealed are suddenly announced out loud to the world; you may lose good friends as a result and promotion could be in jeopardy if baby answers the 'phone when the boss rings. Young children, since they have memories of such phenomenal depth, make elephants look like amnesiacs, so be prepared for twenty years or more of this in front of you.

Invent a code to use in conversation around the house. We used to spell things backwards, but when one day I said: 'I really don't think I can stand the whole day with e–i–t–n–u–a e–n–i–l–u–a–p', and Tom said: 'No, I don't like Auntie Pauline much either', we suddenly realised he had twigged years ago, which is probably why he's now brilliant at spelling, albeit backwards.

One Christmas some good friends of ours bought their boy one of those children's big plastic tape-recorders, and this simple act of parental generosity nearly proved their downfall. They had some Nameless Friends who constantly asked them to babysit but rarely offered to do the same. Because their children all got on so well together our friends decided simply to put up with the Nameless Couple but one day, when asked yet again to help out, they both exploded with anger and ranted and raged at each other about the appalling selfish behaviour of the Nameless Couple, how it was time all this had to stop, why couldn't they see how bloody unreasonable they were being towards us? God damn them both to hell etc. etc.

By the next evening, when the Nameless Couple were due round to drop off their children yet again, our friends had calmed down a little and agreed that they would make one final effort to be polite and civil. They were sitting in the kitchen having a stiff g. and t. when, to their absolute horror, their little lad appeared just as the Nameless Couple's car had crunched up onto the drive of their house. In his little hand was the tape-recorder, turned to full volume, and the words that emerged from it were of a certain familiarity. The little urchin had recorded the rantings of the previous evening in their entirety and as he entered the kitchen they could hear something along the lines of 'That miserable bloody Nameless Couple, I've really had enough of their conniving f---ing ways, that's it, I hate the bastards . . . .' etc. etc. The consequences of their boy walking into the kitchen thirty seconds later, or the Nameless Couple arriving thirty seconds earlier are, they assure me, too painful even to contemplate.

Father's Traditional Duty upon arriving home in the evening, of course, is Reading The Bedtime Story and I'm convinced this has made a bigger contribution to extending the children's vocabulary than anything else. It certainly has mine. After reading all those Mr Men books by that bloke Roger Hargreaves over and over again, words like jealousy, envy, invidious and covetousness start floating to mind. Mr Hargreaves used to be in advertising and spent his days commuting backwards and forwards to some dreary office in Town. He can't draw and writes in sentences of stunning simplicity but my children adore those bloody books and Mr Hargreaves is now a millionaire living in tax exile in Jersey. Yes, reading those night after night after night after an exhausting day in the office in London has increased my vocabulary all right.

It is tiring enough reading stories of numbing familiarity but, very early on, Tom and Alex started to demand that I made up stories to tell them rather than just pick them out of a book and this has aged me by years. The trouble is that they insist on so many conditions and inclusions in the plot that the process of inventing a credible story becomes exhausting.

FATHER'S TRADITIONAL DUTY UPON ARRIVING HOME IN THE EVENING OF COURSE, IS READING THE BEDTIME STORY.

The fundamental error, I realised much later, was in ever asking the initial question: 'What would you like the story to be about?' Don't ever ask this question, because if you do a discussion along the following lines will ensue:

'What would you like the story to be about tonight?'

'A Teddy-Bear!'

'Right. Once upon a time, a Teddy-Bear called Peter –'

'– called Jimmy – '

'– a Teddy-Bear called Jimmy, who lived with his –'

'– pet whale –'

'– pet whale?'

'– pet whale!'

'– called Jimmy, who lived with his pet whale –'

'– called Henrietta –'

'– called Henrietta, near a huge –'

'– swimming pool –'

'– near a huge swimming pool, decided that his –'

'– tummy hurt –'

'– tummy hurt?' etc. etc.

Now I don't know whether you have ever had to put forward a convincing story line about a Teddy Bear called Jimmy with an upset tummy who lived with his pet whale Henrietta beside a swimming pool but I can tell you that, at 7 p.m. after a hard day's work, it can do considerable long-term damage to one's creative potential.

Don't be alarmed if your child becomes totally single-minded about something. Tom, for example, became obsessed with volcanoes whilst still only two. I think he had seen a particularly vivid picture of a volcano exploding in one of his ABC books and the image must have been so compelling that it has remained with him for years. He seemed to be both attracted by the power of the things yet repelled and frightened by them at the same time, often waking in the middle of the night after a terrible dream in which a volcano had exploded right slap bang in the middle of our vegetable patch, covering the entire village with a combination of bubbling hot lava and roasted runner-beans.

Yet despite this, his total fascination with volcanoes meant he kept on and on badgering us for more information about them and, eventually we found an encyclopaedia of volcanoes with a large selection of stunning photographs complete with long and detailed histories into which he threw himself with a passionate intensity. At bedtimes – and every other time of day come to that – he would demand we read out the case studies of the world's great volcanic eruptions over and over and over again until we, like him, gradually became experts on the whole subject. Were you even now to casually drop the words Siretoko-Iwo-Zan into the conversation, for example, I would come straight back at you like a squash-ball fired from a rifle with: '5,000 foot Japanese strato-volcano active as a solfatara noted for the 200,000 tons of almost pure sulphur produced after the lateral phreatic explosion of 1936' and probably be unable to restrain the look of surprise on my face that you appeared unaware of these very basic facts yourself. Tom would, too.

Thanks no doubt to a particularly graphic drawing, the explosions of Krakatoa (originally consisting, as I'm sure you know, of three volcanic cones around a submerged caldera situated directly above huge deposits of gaseous pyromagma and supersaturated hypomagma) off the coast of Java a hundred years ago took pride of place in Tom's mind. He could rattle off details about Krakatoa with the speed other children could recite 'Baa Baa Black Sheep'. Friends and relatives would be stunned when he'd toddle over to them with conversational openers like: 'The main 1883 eruption of the Krakatoa archipelago stimulated one of the largest tsunamis the world has ever seen, you know Granny', or: 'Did you know, Auntie Pauline, that 36,000 people drowned when the tsunami swept across the city of Telok Betong?' On shopping expeditions to the supermarket he would waltz up to total strangers and ask them for the precise date of Krakatoa's third great eruption. 'And I want the month as well as the year', he'd demand of some poor bemused pensioner struggling to fill up a brown paper bag with carrots.

* * *

If and when your child starts behaving like this, you may find it diverting to try to work out exactly who he or she was in their previous lives. Those convinced by the theory of reincarnation argue that the behaviour of babies and very small children are absolute proof that we have all existed as human beings before. 'After all,' said Voltaire, 'It is no more surprising to be born twice than it is to be born once.'

For example, a Danish toddler called Christian Friedrich Heinecken is said to have talked within a few hours of his birth in 1721, an astonishing feat for totally undeveloped vocal chords which was probably the origin of the well-known Danish maxim about Heinecken refreshing the parts others can't reach. By the age of two, this precocious child knew the whole of Biblical history; at three he was extremely familiar with both world history and world geography while speaking fluent Latin, French and German; at four he died. Wolfgang Amadeus Mozart wrote minuets, a piano concerto and a sonata when aged four; at seven he composed a full-length opera. An article in a 1928 edition of the *British Journal of Psychical Research* featured a two-year-old Mexican called Miguel Mantilla who, within fifteen seconds, could answer questions like: 'In what years will February 4th be a Friday?' and 'What date was the second Sunday in 1840?' And so it goes on, endless lists of children who apparently have a knowledge which they would have been quite incapable of absorbing in their own short lives. The catalogue goes right up to the present day. In 1971, for example, Frank de Felitta and his wife Dorothy were in the garden of their Los Angeles home when they suddenly heard brilliant ragtime piano-playing coming from their house. Rushing inside they found their six-year-old son Raymond at the keyboard of the family piano that he had never even attempted to play before. His playing went on to be hailed as brilliant right across the United States.

Julius Caesar believed in it; so did Frederick the Great. The oil billionaire, J. Paul Getty, thought he was once the Roman Emperor Hadrian, the actress Shirley Maclaine is convinced she was a dancer in an Egyptian harem, whilst the Buddhist Old Bailey judge Christmas Humphries believed he was sentenced to death over 3,000 years ago during the reign of Rameses II for making love to a Virgin of Isis, a girl priest who had sworn to refrain from sex.

My own thoughts on this are in line with those of Sir Winston Churchill. 'It is conceivable that I might well be reborn as a Chinese coolie', said Churchill. 'In such a case I should lodge a protest.' If however you feel there may be something in it then buy a piano or, better still, ask your two-year-old in what years February 4th will be a Friday and see what happens.

On the other hand, watching your child dribble, belch, throw its food around, abuse everyone in sight, fart and have tantrums may well prompt the question: 'Has he inherited all his characteristics directly from me?' The honest answer is probably yes, without exception, although scientifically there has been a good deal of argument over the years about how much a child's personality – particularly his IQ – is developed by your genes, and how much by the environ-

HAS HE INHERITED ALL HIS CHARACTERISTICS DIRECTLY FROM YOU?

ment in which the child grows up.

The eminent Professor Herrnstein from Harvard University, for example, carried out a detailed history of intelligence testing and came to the firm conclusion that up to 90 per cent of intelligence is determined by heredity. The equally eminent Professor Kamin, on the other hand, from the equally famous Princeton University, carried out an equally detailed analysis of the inheritability of IQ and came to the firm conclusion that Professor Herrnstein's firm conclusion was a load of old cobblers and that there was no reliable data proving that IQ had anything whatsoever to do with heredity.

Right, said Prof. Herrnstein's camp, what we will do is prove you wrong by tracking down sets of identical twins who have been separated and reared apart and compare their IQs. Since identical twins have identical genes this should settle the argument once and for all. The result, they said, showed incontrovertibly that there was a very strong similarity in the IQs of identical twins reared apart, so there.

'Honestly!' said Prof. Kamin's camp, 'Are you stupid or something?' He accused them of biased testing and drew attention to the very similar environments in which the twins were reared, where often the children were placed in the homes of relatives or friends of exactly the same socio-economic status.

As a basic rule of thumb, then, make sure that at dinner parties you quote Prof. Herrnstein if your child is obviously outstanding, and Prof. Kamin if he's not, remembering of course to blame it all instead on the inadequacies of the play-school teacher.

8

FOR THE REST OF YOUR DAYS . . .

Kronus, the son of Uranus, had a habit of devouring his children and I must say there are times in the day when I have a degree of sympathy with his point of view. Children have an unswerving ability to locate your most vulnerable point and gnaw away at it until you are driven quite insane. Is this subconsciously because they like the idea of living with barmy parents? Possibly, although it is more likely that they know instinctively that most of us shun the prospect of insanity and, rather than concede to it, eventually give way to their demands.

Mind you, poor old Kronus did have problems of his own. After marrying his own sister, Rhea, he then went ahead and castrated his father, which in my opinion was rather overdoing things; had he been around these days he would no doubt have been eligible for a local authority grant to form his own self-help group.

In my world there is one place where this nasty streak in my children is more likely to appear than any other. Over the months it is a place which they have visited with me a good deal because, in our household, it is father who often takes them there, and now even the remote prospect of me having to visit it is sufficient to send spiky shudders up and down the old spinal column like the sparks from a huge catherine-wheel.

It is the waiting-room in the village surgery.

Being a small Hampshire practice with its own dispensary and of course, only one doctor, the waiting-room is the size of a modest shower-cubicle, nearly always crammed with highly infectious patients who arrive with one unpleasant complaint and leave with quite another. The problem is that, while we all huddle together sneezing, coughing and scratching the time away until summoned by Dr Truscott, Tom and Alex never, ever stop talking; not ordinary conversation, you understand, but talk spiced with as much wickedness and malice as they feel sufficient to create the maximum amusement from the captive audience and maximum humiliation to Yours Faithfully.

They first discovered the sadistic potential of such a snug, ready-made stage when I took along Alex, who was suffering from earache. I'm told other children with earache become quiet and morose; I'd never known Alex so perky. After a few minutes of very conspicuous, thorough inspection of a patient opposite suffering from acute acne she asked, piercingly: 'Daddy, why has that man got such a horrible spotty face?' The poor fellow did his best to shrink behind a copy of *Knitting World* and so did I.

'Daddy, didn't you hear me? Why has that man got such a horrible spotty face?'

'Alex, look at the *Beano*!'

'What's wrong with it? It's horrible!'

'Alex, look at the *Beano*!'

Alex had a good deal of earache that winter. A week later we were back and this time I noticed, with growing nervousness, her attention was immediately drawn to a strangely hermaphroditic creature with elaborate ear-rings, a thin moustache, a very large bosom and a savage crew-cut, two seats down.

'Alex, have you seen this week's new *Beano*?'

'Daddy . . . .'

'It looks really good, look at that funny blue elephant on the front . . . .'

'Daddy!'

'Yes, dear?'

'Is that a man or a lady sitting over there?'

Her words hung in the air for a moment. Several people bit their lips. I bit my lip. Alex was waiting for an answer, and she wasn't going to wait long.

Suddenly the hermaphrodite looked and, in an extraordinarily deep voice like Al Jolson's, announced: 'Lots of people aren't sure, lovey', and, slapping its thigh like a lumberjack, it then roared with laughter. Everyone else started to laugh, too. Except me.

The following week Tom caught Alex's ear infection. I don't know whether she'd had a quiet word with him beforehand but I noticed that when we sat down in the waiting-room Tom had an evil twinkle in his eye. I began to feel uncomfortable.

'Daddy.'

'Yes.'

'I like your anorak.'

This did not bode well. I had an idea what might be coming but there was nothing I could do. Quickly I reached for the latest edition of *Knitting World*. Everyone else shuffled with anticipation.

'Daddy.'

'Yes.'

'It's MUCH nicer than the last one.'

'Good.'

I had never known such an excruciating silence.

'Daddy.'

'Yes.'

'Do you remember, Mummy didn't like the first one you

DADDY, IS THAT A MAN OR A LADY?

bought, did she?'

'No.'

'Do you remember that?'

'Yes.'

Another ghastly pause.

'Daddy, do you remember, Mummy made you take that one back to the shop and change it, didn't she Daddy?'

'Yes.'

'Do you remember, she said she wouldn't be seen dead with you in that anorak, didn't she Daddy?'

'Well . . . .'

'Daddy.'

'Yes?'

'What does "appalling taste" mean?'

And so on, in a state of permanent, nightmarish agony. And it isn't just the waiting-room. Oh, no! The other day, in the newsagents, Alex asked the shop assistant if she was wearing underpants and Tom demanded to know who the post-mistress was sleeping with.

* * *

And yet, although they would never admit it, it is quite astonishing how much loyalty children really have towards their parents. Recently I spent a week at a children's home making a documentary. There were over forty children there, aged from five to eighteen, all of them the victim of some terrible domestic crisis that was so serious the social services had felt compelled to remove them from their homes completely – not a step taken lightly. Superficially these children appeared perfectly normal and your first impression upon walking into the place was: 'What on earth are all these kids actually here for?' After a time, though, as you grew to know them, the scars that they each held just beneath the surface gradually began to emerge. These were the children of drug addicts, prostitutes, thieves, child-beaters, the mentally ill and yet, from every single child, shone one burning desire: to go home. No matter how badly they had been treated in the past, their mums, their dads, were the finest in the world.

It was quite a revelation.

The staff at the children's home took me quite by surprise, too, as it happens, as they struggled to walk the thin line between giving emotional support to their charges without becoming emotionally involved. They were outstanding. Mind you, once a week, on a Wednesday, a psychiatrist visited the home and, when I enquired how many of the children he managed to see on each visit, I was politely informed that he was here to see members of staff, not the children.

Sooner or later your child will begin to become very inquisitive about your job – that is, if you have one. What on earth does Daddy get up to all that time during the day? Who is it that is so much more fun to be with than Mummy and me? These are questions Mummy may well have been asking, too.

Although I spend most of my working life as a freelance radio and television journalist, my most dubious claim to fame comes through winning endless Golden Egg Awards on the BBC's *Late Late Breakfast Show* for a horrifying piece of film in which a sex-starved pig attempts to tear off my testicles. This appalling footage has now been shown on television so often that both my children are convinced that I actually earn a living by being savaged by wild animals. In fact it seems pretty bizarre to me, too, that I have become best-known for a series of frightful cock-ups and out-takes

BOTH MY CHILDREN ARE CONVINCED THAT I EARN A LIVING BY BEING SAVAGED BY WILD ANIMALS.

that were never intended to be shown in the first place. I have now been on so often that my children express astonishment when told that the fathers of other children don't have mantelpieces full of Golden Egg Awards, and assume that all fathers, when going shopping or buying drinks at the pub or going for a walk in the park are greeted by people pointing and poking each other in the ribs, hoots of laughter, and cries of 'Hey Martha! There's that geezer what had his wotsits nipped off by that bleedin' porker!'

The questions don't get any easier, either. Tom and Alex ask their most profound questions first thing in the morning, because they have been up most of the night pondering over them. In fact we spent most of last winter on British Summer Time. For six months both the children resolutely refused to adjust to the fact that the clocks had gone back an hour, and both continued to wake me up at 6 a.m. sharp, normally with an extremely profound question which, at that time of day, I'm completely unable to answer. Come to think of it, I'm completely unable to answer them at any time of day. The answers to queries like: 'Why don't cows ever wipe their bottoms?' and, on a roughly similar theme: 'Why don't people in cartoons ever go to the lavatory?' can prove strangely elusive at first light.

Last week Tom – who is now five – woke me up with this little poser:

'Daddy, who made God?'

Now I'd had quite a heavy evening the night before and anyway I'm more used to being woken up with soothing music or a little lighthearted banter on the radio. Even so, I had to be impressed.

'Did you think that out for yourself, or did you hear someone else ask it?'

'I thought it out for myself because God couldn't make himself, could he?'

I considered this. 'No, I suppose not. Anyway, it's a good question?'

'Why's it a good question?'

'Because no one knows the answer.'

It was Tom's turn to ponder for a moment.

'Not even Uncle Richard?' he finally asked.

'Not even Uncle Richard.'

* * *

Over the years your children will gradually, inexorably, alter your entire personality. For example, you will almost certainly experience a total loss of ambition. Don't be alarmed by this, it has happened to the best of us. I used to be obsessed with the idea of one day getting my own network television programme at peak viewing seven nights a week. I planned to own at least two Mercedes by the time I was twenty, write my first best-seller by the time I was twenty-five, and have my own tennis court and swimming pool with holidays annually at my own holiday homes in Gstaad, Barbados and California by the age of thirty.

I'm now thirty-three and I can't stop thinking about when I can next get into the potting-shed to complete the latest batch of elderberry wine; having a good time is planting the runner beans and the ultimate satisfaction is seeing Tom and Alex come in the first three in the egg-and-spoon race at the village show.

There is a man I used to know who had a reputation for being a bit of a bastard at work. Actually he had a bit of a reputation for being a bit of a bastard at home, too, but that's another story. Rich, well-cut suit. Rich, well-fed face. Own business, stand no nonsense in the office, I only employ the best here, if you're not up to scratch you can go and pick your nose on the dole queue.

Nice sort of fella.

He had a little girl a few years ago. One Christmas I sat next to him at the play-school Nativity Play. Every drying-up cloth within a five-mile radius of the village had been purloined to make head-dresses for all the Arab shepherds and wise men. There were more children than there were parts so some of the smaller ones played sheep or donkeys, or even more demanding roles like trees, or passing clouds.

I thought, rather optimistically in retrospect I suppose, that the children would re-enact the story of the birth of Christ, but this wasn't the case at all. One by one each of the children simply came to the front of the stage and did a turn; the older children sang carols and the younger ones sang anything they could remember.

This chap's daughter came on near the end. I remember her vividly, even now, that tiny little three-year-old face tight with nerves, with a big black moustache painted on in felt-tip and a red-and-green striped drying-up cloth hanging over her head. She sang 'Hickory-Dickory-Dock' which, since she was supposed to be the Bethlehem innkeeper, didn't seem to be terribly appropriate to the Christmas Story; I say sang, she was actually so nervous she whispered it so that the whole hall fell into an eerie silence as she spoke.

When she finally managed to reach the end of the verse, after several hiccups, stops and starts and half a dozen prompts, the hall exploded into rapturous applause.

I shall never forget the look of burning pride on that man's face.

All of which prompts a question which, despite my very best researches and endeavours, I have so far been quite unable to answer. I have looked high and low, left no stone unturned, sought in every corner, however dark; and yet I

THE QUESTION IS THIS: WHAT THE DEVIL DO PEOPLE WHO DON'T HAVE CHILDREN DO ALL DAY?

am no nearer enlightenment. The enigma remains, the answer locked forever just out of reach, the door eternally barred and bolted.

The question is this: 'What the devil do people who don't have children DO all day?'

Alas, it is far too late for me to find that out now. I shall never know.